WHAT GOD HAS SAID

ABOUT THE

Holy Spirit

LENN ZELLER

*And the life and power He brings
to those who believe*

What God Has Said—About the Holy Spirit
AND THE LIFE AND POWER HE BRINGS
TO THOSE WHO BELIEVE
by Lenn Zeller

Copyright © 2022

All rights reserved. No part of this book may be used or reproduced by any means, graphic, electronic, or mechanical, including photocopying, recording, taping or by any information storage retrieval system without the written permission of the author except in the case of brief quotations embodied in critical articles and reviews.

This book is a work of non-fiction. Unless otherwise noted, the author and the publisher make no explicit guarantees as to the accuracy of the information contained in this book and in some cases, names of people and places have been altered to protect their privacy.

Because of the dynamic nature of the Internet, any web addresses or links contained in this book may have changed since publication and may no longer be valid. The views expressed in this work are solely those of the author and do not necessarily reflect the views of the publisher, and the publisher hereby disclaims any responsibility for them.

Scripture quotations taken from The Holy Bible, New International Version® NIV® Copyright © 1973 1978 1984 2011 by Biblica, Inc. TM. Used by permission. All rights reserved worldwide.

Library of Congress Number: 2022942586
International Standard Book Number: 978-1-60126-811-2

Masthof Press
219 Mill Road | Morgantown, PA 19543-9516
www.Masthof.com

DEDICATION

*Dedicated to the glory of God the Father,
Son and Holy Spirit*

Table of Contents

INTRODUCTION | vii

CHAPTER 1   *Hovering Over the Waters* 1

CHAPTER 2   *The Spirit on Them* 11

CHAPTER 3   *Where Can I Go From Your Spirit?* 22

CHAPTER 4   *A New Spirit in You* 32

CHAPTER 5   *I Will Pour Out My Spirit* 43

CHAPTER 6   *By My Spirit* 53

CHAPTER 7   *A Spirit of Grace and Supplication* 64

CHAPTER 8   *The Spirit of Your Father* 73

CHAPTER 9   *The Spirit Gives Birth to Spirit* 81

CHAPTER 10   *Another Counselor* 93

CHAPTER 11   *Teacher and Reminder* 102

CHAPTER 12   *The One Who Convicts and Convinces* 113

CONCLUSION | 122

ENDNOTES | 125

APPENDIX | 131

ABOUT THE AUTHOR | 133

ALSO BY LENN ZELLER | 134

Introduction

Showing my age, I remember a television commercial for a certain asset management firm which used to intone: "When ---- speaks, everyone listens." And on the screen you would see people suddenly stopping whatever they were doing to hear what was spoken by this supposedly trusted, revered source of reliable financial wisdom. It was an advertising campaign that ran for quite a long time because it effectively convinced people that this particular firm knew what they were doing and could be counted on to invest your hard earned money in a beneficial and profitable way.

Certainly we want to be sure to listen to sources in all areas of life that we can depend on to give us accurate, truthful information. No one with any common sense intentionally seeks out advice that they assume will be wrong. There are times, of course, when those we trust will be mistaken or ill-informed, and then the result for us can be difficult or even disastrous. But, for the most part, we try to follow the advice of people whom we think will give us sound counsel.

Where can we turn to receive truthful, solid answers to questions of a spiritual nature? Who can best tell us about eternal things of the soul, about meaning and purpose, about God and our relationship with Him? People turn in a variety of directions: friends, horoscopes, tarot cards, psychics, internet sites or television preachers.

Ultimately, there is only one truly reliable and infallible source—God Himself. God is the Creator and Sustainer of all that is. God is the source and fountainhead of all truth, wisdom, and knowledge, and the One who holds all the mysteries of life in His own counsel.

"To God belong wisdom and power;
counsel and understanding are His." (Job 12:13)

So if you want to know who God is, who better to give you an accurate and true portrait than God Himself? That was the focus of my first book in this series: *"What God Has Said—About God."* Take that a step further: if you want to know who and what *Jesus* is, who better to tell you than God? That was the focus of the next volume: *"What God Has Said—About Jesus."*

In *this* one we will turn to a consideration of the *Holy Spirit*. Who is He? What does He do? How can we know more of Him and relate better to Him? Once again, we will turn to God for the answers. And, as before, we will focus on passages in the Bible in which God Himself tells us something about the Holy Spirit.

As before, this will not be an attempt at a complete systematic Biblical theology of the Spirit. We will simply focus our attention on a few specific passages from God's Word in which He directly told us something about the third person of the Trinity. I will leave it up to you to do a more thorough study of the topic on your own. Perhaps these pages will stimulate you to do so.

When it comes to the Holy Spirit, I would suggest that many Christians tend to one of two extremes. On the one end of the spectrum are some believers who give little or no consideration to the Holy Spirit, preferring to focus mostly on the Father and the Son, which to them are much more tangible and understandable. Yes, there is the Spirit of God, but Who He is and how we can best relate to Him are bewildering issues that are best kept at a distance from the realities of daily life.

To make matters worse, He was at one time popularly referred to as the "Holy Ghost," and still is in some quarters. To some—such as to me, as a child at least—even a "Holy Ghost" carries a connotation of a phantom, specter or apparition, like Casper or Ghost Busters. That gives rise to thoughts of a haunting, prowling or frightening otherworldly being, not an image that welcomes or draws people to Him.

At the other end of the theological continuum are those who consider the Holy Spirit to be the end all and be all of any life of true faith, and consider those who are not as "charismatic" or "Spirit-filled" as they are to be not even truly saved believers. If you don't speak in tongues and experience ecstatic worship, then your faith is woefully inadequate—if real at all.

A fellow pastor once invited us to dinner. In the ensuing conversation, he spent a considerable amount of time explaining to us his Pentecostal theology and implying that anything different ("less" would have been his term for it) simply is not adequate. And he never failed to privately and publicly, condescendingly and unequivocally, point out that our church (and its pastor!) was simply not up to the level of spiritual maturity of his—because we were not Pentecostal enough, in his opinion. Sometimes people are quite strident about their views concerning the Holy Spirit and our relationship to Him.

So how are we to navigate this divide in a reasonable way? My proposal for a place to begin is to listen to what God the Father Himself has to say about God the Spirit. That will be our starting place in this volume. Hopefully, these discussions will inspire further study and discussions as we seek to grow in knowledge and wisdom.

CHAPTER 1

Hovering Over the Waters

"In the beginning God created the heavens and the earth. Now the earth was formless and empty, darkness was over the surface of the deep, and the Spirit of God was hovering over the waters." (Genesis 1:1-2)

In the beginning—God. God: the Supreme Being; *Elohim*, signifying in the Hebrew "Strong" and "Mighty." It is expressive of omnipotent power and capacity.[1] It is also plural, by the way, speaking of God the Trinity—Father, Son and Spirit; as highlighted in Genesis 1:26, when God said: *"Let Us make man in Our image, in Our likeness"* (Genesis 1:26, emphasis mine). God is plural, three distinct Persons in one divine Being.

"In the beginning"—God. With this dramatic and profound phrase the Bible opens. This is the sacred, eternal, infallible, universal, unchanging, holy, written Word of the one true God. And its beginning is about the beginning. But what does that mean?

In my younger (and less serious) years, I would sometimes tell a corny Biblical joke: Did you know that baseball is mentioned in the Bible? It is. Genesis 1:1—"In the big inning." I know, I know, juvenile. And, to be clear, this iconic phrase is *not* about baseball, much as some of us may enjoy playing and watching that particular sport.

"In the beginning" refers to an age before time itself, before creation, "a period of remote and unknown antiquity, hid in the depths of eternal ages."[2] This was the nothingness from which God created everything that is, somewhere in infinity past. As it is used in Proverbs 8:22-23, where Wisdom is speaking:

1

> *"The LORD brought me forth as the first of His works, before*
>   *His deeds of old;*
> *I was appointed from eternity, from the beginning, before the*
>   *world began."*

From the beginning, before the world began. That's what we're talking about here, before anything other than God Himself existed.

Why is there something rather than nothing? This is the primary question of philosophy. How did something come out of this dark, formless, emptiness of unknown antiquity? It came from the infinite wisdom and power of God. God spoke, and it came into being. This universe and all that exists did not somehow spring up out of the "primordial ooze." There *was* no ooze from which creation could develop. There were no extraterrestrials flying in to create life on this planet, as some have postulated in a desperate and ridiculous attempt to deny the existence of God. There was no "Big Bang," as others insist. There was nothing to explode and nothing from which an explosion could bring the universe into existence. The Hebrew word for "formless" (*tohu*) means: *confusion, unreality, emptiness* and *chaos*.[3] There was absolute desolation and oblivion—until God spoke and created.

In the beginning God created the heavens and the earth.

> *"Blessed is he whose help is the God of Jacob,*
> *whose hope is in the LORD his God,*
> *the Maker of heaven and earth,*
> *the sea, and everything in them—*
> *the LORD, who remains faithful forever." (Psalm 146:5-6)*

It was God who made heaven and earth, the sea and everything in them. He made them *ex nihilo*—out of nothing. Only God can make something out of nothing, simply by the command of His Word.

There's an old parable of sorts in which God challenges a disbelieving scientist to create life. The scientist says, "OK, I'll just take some of this seawater." God says, "Whoa, I made that seawater, make your own." So the scientist takes some mud, and God says, "No, I made that mud. Make your own. You need to start from absolutely nothing, like I did." The point being, only God can make something—much less life—out of nothing!

"And the Spirit of God was hovering over the waters." (Genesis 1:2). There we have the first mention of the Holy Spirit. But from whom does this mention come? The Old Testament book of Genesis, in both Scripture itself (Nehemiah 13:1; Luke 24:27; John 5:46; and others) and in church tradition, is attributed to Moses, along with the whole of the Pentateuch—the first five Old Testament books, Genesis through Deuteronomy.[4] There are many who would argue that point, claiming it is a composite of the writings of several ancient authors, quoting numerous prehistoric sources, none of whom was Moses, over a period of some four or five hundred years.

We are here going to assume that Moses did indeed write the Pentateuch, as Jesus confirmed (Luke 24:44 and others). But then we must wonder—how would Moses know about creation itself or about the Spirit of God hovering over that vast expanse of nothingness? That was long before Moses was even born. How could he so dramatically describe events that took place centuries before his birth?

The answer to that has to do with the divine inspiration of Scripture. Moses was the *human* author of Genesis, but he wrote under the *inspiration* of God Himself. As Paul wrote to Timothy:

"All Scripture is God-breathed and is useful for teaching, rebuking, correcting and training in righteousness so that the man of God may be thoroughly equipped for every good work." (2 Timothy 3:16-17)

Some translations, such as the King James Version and the New American Standard Bible, say that the Bible was "inspired" by God. But I don't think that description goes far enough. That could imply simply that God gave the idea, or that God motivated or stirred the humans to write, but they did so mostly from their own experience, beliefs and the understandings of their day, age and culture.

Somewhat like my writing of this (and my previous) books. I was in some sense "inspired" to do some writing after I retired from parish ministry. Was it God who provided that stimulus or was it my own personal, inner urges? I can't say for sure, but I would like to think it was God's idea. Or at least perhaps He used my own thoughts and dreams to prompt me to do something He had in mind for me all along.

But did God *breathe* these words into me like He did for Moses and the other authors of Scripture? I would say most assuredly not. I make no claim to inerrancy or divine authorship here.

That would be because to say that Scripture was "God-Breathed," which is closer to the original language, goes much deeper than a mere stimulation or encouragement to put pen to paper, or quill to scroll, as the case may be. It means God breathed into Moses and the other human authors His own eternal Word. It means that Scripture, unlike this book, has a divine origin, and comes directly from the mind and Spirit of God Himself, from which arise all claims to its veracity, reliability, timelessness, inerrancy and crucial importance for life and faith.

Our text is a classic case in point. Genesis 1:1 is not the words or mind of Moses. It cannot possibly be so, because it describes things that happened long before Moses' time. These words were breathed out from God. God gave this to Moses in a very profound, personal and direct way. And therefore, when the text says that the Spirit hovered over the waters at the beginning of creation, we can realistically say that these are the words of God.

Now, the question has been raised, if all was nothingness and emptiness, over what was the Holy Spirit hovering? I think most likely it was as one commentator suggested: in this "undescribed period" God had already called into being the globe which would become earth. It was a dark and watery waste, till out of this chaotic state, the present fabric of the world was made to arise.[5]

Another commentator says,

> *"Here is the work of creation in its embryo, where we have an account of the first matter and the first mover. A chaos was the first matter. It is here called the earth ... it is also called the deep, both for its vastness and because the waters which were afterwards separated from the earth were now mixed with it. This immense mass of matter was it out of which all bodies, even the firmament and visible heavens themselves, were afterwards produced by the power*

of the Eternal Word. The Creator could have made His work perfect at first, but by this gradual proceeding He would show what is, ordinarily, the method of His providence and grace."[6]

What does all that mean? Best I can understand, God the Father, Son and Spirit was in the process of creation. Out of nothing He called this vast, formless chaos into existence, from which everything else would follow according to His Word of command.

And in the midst of all this creative activity, what did God say, through His prophet Moses, about the Holy Spirit? He said that *"the Spirit of God was hovering over the waters."* So that is where we will begin our current study. The Hebrew means to move gently, cherish and hover.[7] As another commentary says it, the Spirit of God literally continued to brood over it, as a bird does when hatching eggs.[8] In Deuteronomy 32, Scripture speaks of:

> *"an eagle that stirs up its nest and hovers over its young, that spreads its wings to catch them and carries them on its pinions."*
> *(Deuteronomy 32:11)*

What a wonderful word picture that is! That's the sense of this word.

A robin built her nest on a metal I-beam under our deck this past spring. We enjoyed watching her brood over her eggs, then saw her hover over and feed her young as they grew and matured. And we saw the chicks reach the point of leaving the nest and taking their first tentative flight. But even then the hovering of the mother over her chicks did not end. We watched the chicks hopping around the yard looking for things to eat (bugs or worms, maybe?), but staying close to the mother and carefully keeping her in sight all the while; as she also carefully watched over them. There was gentleness in her care for her young, and even, I might say, a sense of cherishing them.

In a similar way, the Spirit of God gently and carefully hovered over the face of the deep during the creative work of the divine Trinity. This hovering over the void by the Holy Spirit was not a passive thing. He was not mindlessly lounging there, absently viewing the creation come into being. It describes a very active, dynamic, lively participation with God the Father and God the Son in the action of creation. As in Psalm 33:

> *"By the word of the LORD were the heavens made,*
> *their starry host by the breath of His mouth."* (Psalm 33:6)

The word translated there as "breath" is the same word that is used often in Scripture for "Spirit," affirming the participation of the Spirit in God's work of creation.

So what has God the Father said about the Holy Spirit? He said, in essence, in Genesis 1:2—"The Spirit is My Partner and Co-Creator. He was there and was active in our work from the beginning." This is an affirmation of the orthodox Christian doctrine of the trinity. In the beginning God created the heavens and the earth. But the Holy Spirit was actively present and joining in that glorious work.

And Jesus was there and active as well:

> *"In the beginning was the Word, and the Word was with God, and the Word was God. He was with God in the beginning. Through Him all things were made; without Him nothing was made that has been made."* (John 1:1-3)

"The Word" is a reference to Jesus. All things were made through Jesus and apart from Jesus nothing was made. So we can easily see that Father, Son and Spirit were active collaborators in the work of creation. It was a joint effort, in which each of the three persons of the Trinity had a hand, including the Holy Spirit, as the third person of that divine Threesome.

This text also illustrates the infinite presence and being of the Spirit. God had no beginning and has no end. He has always existed in the infinite past, and He will always exist into the eternal future. The Westminster Shorter Catechism states that "God is a spirit, infinite, eternal and unchangeable in His being."

> *"Praise be to the LORD, the God of Israel,*
> *from everlasting to everlasting."* (1 Chronicles 16:36)

> *"Now to the King eternal, immortal, invisible, the only God, be honor and glory for ever and ever. Amen."* (1 Timothy 1:17)

From everlasting to everlasting, eternal and immortal—God is infinite and eternal, as are the Spirit and the Son. "So it is as we would expect: if all three members of the Trinity are equally and fully divine [as we believe they are], then all three have existed for all eternity, and God has eternally existed as a Trinity."[9]

Before the existence of time itself, before the creation of the heavens and the earth, when the only thing that existed was God Himself, the Holy Spirit was there, eventually hovering over the formless void and assisting in the act of creation. Infinitely into the past the Spirit has been. Eternally into the future, the Spirit will be.

Do you think of the Holy Spirit as eternally existent or do you think of Him in mostly the present tense, as the Helper and Counselor promised by Jesus to assist believers during the age of the church? Do you imagine His work being exclusively during this present age, since the day of Pentecost?

The presence and the work of the Holy Spirit can be seen all throughout Scripture, from this very beginning of time and matter (and before), on through the centuries of God's people. Back in the days preceding the great flood which covered the earth and the ark of Noah, God saw the people of earth increasing in number and in sinful depravity. At that early time, the LORD God said:

> *"My Spirit will not contend with man forever, for he is mortal; his days will be a hundred and twenty years." (Genesis 6:3)*

The Holy Spirit was there in the days of Noah, "contending" with humans: executing judgment, governing, even pleading with humankind.[10] This tells us something of the kind of activity in which the Spirit was (and is) engaged in relation to humankind. Again, it is not a passive role, but very vigorous and involved. The Holy Spirit has always been there, drawing people to God and awakening them to the things of the Kingdom.

In the days of Joseph, after he interpreted Pharaoh's dream and suggested a wise course of action to prepare for the coming drought, Pharaoh said:

"Can we find anyone like this man, one in whom is the Spirit of God?" (Genesis 41:38)

Even the pagan Pharaoh could recognize the presence of the Holy Spirit within Joseph, working to infuse him with divine wisdom.

In Numbers 27, when God took Moses up the mountain, giving him a glimpse of the Promised Land and telling Moses that he would soon *"be gathered to [his] people"* (Numbers 27:13), Moses pleaded with God to appoint a new leader over the people *"to go out and come in before them, one who will lead them out and bring them in, so the LORD's people will not be like sheep without a shepherd"* (Numbers 27:16-17). So the LORD said to Moses:

"Take Joshua son of Nun, a man in whom is the Spirit, and lay your hand on him." (Numbers 27:18)

It was the Holy Spirit of God that had prepared Joshua for his role as leader of the people, and who would guide and empower him in the conquest of the Promised Land.

In the days of Micah the prophet, Micah could boldly say:

"But as for me, I am filled with power,
with the Spirit of the LORD,
and with justice and might,
to declare to Jacob his transgression,
to Israel his sin." (Micah 3:8)

The Holy Spirit was present to the prophet in those ancient days, already at work on God's behalf, inspiring and empowering Micah to boldly speak the Word of God to the people of Israel.

Certainly, as we saw above, Moses was a human mentor for Joshua, who learned much just being in the presence of such a God-fearing, faithful man. He was with Moses on numerous occasions when he met with God and received God's guidance. He saw how Moses conducted himself in his relationship with God. He witnessed Moses' manner of leading God's people. How wonderful it was that Joshua had such an opportunity to be trained up in the ways of the LORD.

Who has mentored you? From whom did you learn what it is to be a follower of Christ? Was there someone(s) who invested in you and showed you by their example how to worship and serve the LORD? Please consider thanking them for their intentional or even unintentional influence and expressing the impact they have had in your life.

And beyond that, to whom in your circle of relationships could you offer that kind of caring, mentoring, personal connection? Who could you identify near to you who could benefit from your experience and be encouraged by you in their walk of faith? Ask God to show you how you can be such a personal example and influence to someone else.

A personal mentor of mine, the late Dr. Jacob Wagner, was a faithful pastor and then denominational executive for many years. He made it a point to meet with countless young pastors over the years, individually and also in small group settings, to encourage, guide and even correct them when necessary. I was the beneficiary of his caring concern, as were numerous others he kindly mentored. Whom have you encouraged in a similar way?

Of course, over and above the human mentoring Joshua received from Moses, it was ultimately the Spirit of the living God Who gave him the inner wisdom and courage to follow Moses in the chain of command of God's people. We could go on and on in this vein, highlighting the presence, power and work of the Holy Spirit in and among the people of God. He was always there, as He was before and during creation itself. This first statement from God about the Spirit tells us of His infinite, eternal being and of His cooperative work in creation itself.

QUESTIONS FOR CONTEMPLATION OR CONVERSATION

1. Do you think of the Holy Spirit as eternally existent or do you think of Him in mostly the present tense? Why? How does this affect your understanding of and relationship with Him?

2. Some think of God as the Creator, Jesus as the Savior and the Holy Spirit as the Helper. Does it change your perceptions of God to realize that all three were equally involved in creation? How?

3. Can you think of other occasions in the Old Testament when the Holy Spirit was present and active? List a few, if you can. How does that inform your understanding of who He is?

4. How do you understand the inspiration of Scripture? How does that affect your respect for the Bible and use of it?

5. God had no beginning and will have no end. As you contemplate the eternity of God, what does that inspire within you?

6. We humans have had a beginning, but God has made us to be immortal, with no end. We will either spend eternity with Him in glory, or in endless punishment. How does that make you feel and how do you think about that truth?

CHAPTER 2

The Spirit on Them

"The Lord said to Moses: 'Bring Me seventy of Israel's elders who are known to you as leaders and officials among the people. Have them come to the Tent of Meeting, that they may stand there with you. I will come down and speak with you there, and I will take of the Spirit that is on you and put the Spirit on them. They will help you carry the burden of the people so that you will not have to carry it alone'." (Numbers 11:16-17)

The people of God were on their way to the rich land God had promised them. They had been freed from slavery in Egypt by God's gracious and mighty power. They had escaped Pharaoh's menacing army by divine deliverance. They were guided and protected by God's presence in the pillars of fire and cloud. They were even fed with daily manna from on high. Can you even imagine your daily meals falling from the sky? All was well—so it would have seemed. So it should have been.

But complaints arose and the people murmured, especially, it appears, from the "rabble" with them (as the NIV terms them—not exactly a complimentary descriptive, to be sure). The King James Version calls them *"the mixt multitude."* These were primarily Egyptians: "slaves, persons in the lowest grades of society, partly natives and partly foreigners, bound close to them as companions in misery, and gladly availing themselves of the opportunity to escape in the crowd."[11]

In more modern terminology, we might call them hangers-on, or groupies; outsiders or "au slanders" as in the Pennsylvania Dutch. Exodus

12 tells us that there were six hundred thousand men in the camp, not including women, children and *"many other people"* who went up with them (Exodus 12:37–38). They were people who saw the Israelites escaping the harsh conditions of slavery under the regime of Pharaoh and decided to tag along in order to get away from there themselves. It was their best chance for freedom, and they took it.

But it wasn't long before these very people began to moan and groan. That bland manna stuff was getting tiresome, mundane and dull. It was like coriander seed and looked like resin (Numbers 11:7). I must admit, that does not sound very appetizing to me either. A bit of chocolate mixed in might have helped a lot; at least some dried fruit and nuts for flavor. The people gathered it every day, ground it into a mortar and cooked it in pots or made it into cakes; day after day after day—*ad nauseam*, to some.

What about some meat, they complained? Even as slaves in Egypt we had melons, cucumbers, leaks, onions and garlic—not just this boring, tasteless manna (Numbers 11:4-6). Where's the meat? Do you remember that television advertisement? If you do, you're as old as I am!

Rather than be grateful for what they *did* have out there in the middle of a vast wilderness, they focused on what they *lacked*—something I am prone to quite often myself. How about you? How easy it is for us to be so intensely concentrated on things we want or think we need—the latest model of cell phone, the newest video game, the current shoes or clothes that are the hot item, the car we saw on the street that looked so nice—that we totally lose sight of all the blessings God in His providence *has* given to us. We may even begin to grumble, or even to doubt God's wisdom or love for us.

Sometime ago there appeared in a newspaper a cartoon showing two fields divided by a fence. Both fields were about the same size and each had plenty of the same kind of grass, green and lush.

In each field there was a mule, and each mule had his head through the fence eating grass from the other mule's pasture. All around each mule in his own field was plenty of grass, yet the grass in the other field seemed greener or fresher, although it was harder to get.

And, in the process, the mules were caught in the wires and were unable to extricate themselves. The cartoonist put just one word at the bottom of the picture—"DISCONTENT"![12] How often do we find ourselves at that same place?

It was these "other people" who first began to grumble, but their complaints eventually infected the rest of the camp. Isn't that the normal way of it? How many fine churches have been torn apart when one or two people begin to gripe and whine, often over very insignificant or even imagined matters: getting their feelings hurt over a perceived slight; not being shown what they consider to be proper respect or appreciation; different wishes for how or when to do what within the church; what color carpet the church should install; petty, personal grievances.

And then people begin to express their dissatisfaction. Pretty soon, others take up that refrain. It only takes a spark to get a fire going, as the saying has it, and the division quickly becomes deadly. Many congregations have been destroyed from within by such personal differences. (I might add that Satan is often the unseen force behind such conflict, and rejoices gleefully when his wiles succeed in tearing a church apart.)

Such was the case here. A few grumbled and soon the complaining was widespread. Moses, their leader, heard the bellyaching and became discouraged. He, in turn, complained to God.

> "Why have You brought this trouble on Your servant? What have I done to displease You that You put the burden of all these people on me? Did I conceive all these people? Did I give them birth? Why do You tell me to carry them in my arms, as a nurse carries an infant, to the land You promised on oath to their forefathers? Where can I get meat for all these people? They keep wailing to me, 'Give us meat to eat!' I cannot carry all these people by myself; the burden is too heavy for me. If this is how You are going to treat me, put me to death right now—if I have found favor in Your eyes—and do not let me face my own ruin." (Numbers 11:11-15)

This is too much, he said. I can't do this anymore. How am I supposed to get meat for all these people—there isn't a butcher shop anywhere near us!

Notice that he blamed God for his troubles. Why have *You* brought this trouble upon me? Why have *You* put this burden on my shoulders?

What did I ever do to *You* to make You so displeased with me? So often, in our emotional response to the problems of life, we turn our anger towards God, and put the blame on Him for not giving us what we want and not caring for us as we think He ought.

Besides that, here's a question I have sometimes pondered when reading this. The Exodus 12 passage quoted above tells us that in addition to the six hundred thousand men, plus the women, children and many other people who left Egypt with the Israelites, they took with them *"large droves of livestock, both flocks and herds."* (Exodus 12:38) Endless (it would seem) meat on the hoof. What happened to all those cattle, sheep and goats? Had they already eaten them all? Did they die along the way from lack of water or forage? We aren't told.

What Scripture *does* tell us is that at this point in their journey the people had no food, God provided manna for them and they complained about the limited diet God gave them. And Moses said, "I can't carry this burden by myself. If this is the way it's going to be, just put me to death. I am done."

Have you ever been that discouraged? Have you ever been so frustrated and defeated that you just wanted to die? That is a desperate, lonely and overwhelming place to be. That's where Moses was, and this was relatively early in their journey. "Are we there yet?" the people may have been asking. No, not by a long shot—there was a long journey ahead, in terms of time and distance. Yet Moses was already feeling beaten and crushed by his God-given responsibility, due to the grumbling and complaining of his flock.

It reminds us of the prophet Elijah, after his dramatic showdown with the prophets of Baal, in 1 Kings 18. That was when Elijah challenged the false priests to a contest. They would build an altar and place a sacrifice upon it. Elijah would do the same. They would call on their god, and Elijah would pray to the one true God, to burn the sacrifice with fire from heaven.

The false prophets sang and danced and cut themselves, calling on Baal to light the fire of their altar. Nothing happened (of course). Elijah mocked them and urged them on. They called out all the more—still nothing. But when Elijah prayed, the fire of the Lord fell and burned up the sacrifice on the altar Elijah built for Him, displaying His divine power and might. The people fell on their faces and cried, *"The LORD—He is God! The LORD—He is God!"* (1 Kings 18:39) Then Elijah commanded them to seize the false prophets of Baal, brought them down to the Kishon Valley and slaughtered them there.

That did not go over very well with Queen Jezebel, who had employed and believed in all those false seers; so she pledged to do to Elijah exactly what he had done to them. She threatened his life and pledged vengeance. Elijah fled in terror. Wouldn't you, if the supreme political power of the nation promises violence against you? He ended up hiding in a cave on the sacred mountain of Horeb.

God met him there in a gentle whisper, and asked what he was doing. Elijah replied:

"I have been very zealous for the LORD God Almighty. The Israelites have rejected Your covenant, broken down Your altars, and put Your prophets to death with the sword. I am the only one left, and now they are trying to kill me too." (1 Kings 19:10)

Elijah felt the same sense of overwhelming defeat that Moses was feeling. But God showed him that he was not the only one left who was faithful to God. There was a devoted remnant standing firm in the LORD, in spite of the disbelief of the secular culture around them (sound familiar?). And God sent Elijah off with a call for further ministry.

Likewise, God stepped in to uplift Moses and supply solutions to his dire straits. First, God answered the complaints of the rabble. For the people demanding meat, He promised meat enough for a whole month—enough for them to tire even of that, even to loathe it. Have you ever eaten so much of something, so often, and for so long, that you actually began to detest it? It would be good for me if that worked with Oreo cookies and ice cream (Most any flavor will do but teaberry above all!). Unfortunately, it doesn't work that way for some strange reason. Anyway, God promised a steady diet of meat for one month; but it would be the same meat every day until they came to loathe it. Be careful what you pray for!

As for the weight of leadership on Moses that he was finding so burdensome, God provided help:

> "Bring Me seventy of Israel's elders who are known to you as leaders and officials among the people. Have them come to the Tent of Meeting, that they may stand there with you. I will come down and speak with you there, and I will take of the Spirit that is on you and put the Spirit on them. They will help you carry the burden of the people so that you will not have to carry it alone." (Numbers 11:16-17)

Here again was God the Father speaking in reference to God the Spirit. Moses was to choose seventy elders from among the people, whom he knew to be natural and acknowledged leaders. They were evidently to be men on whom Moses could rely—mature, faithful and stable men who could be trusted with the responsibility of spiritual leadership. It appears that these were men who already had some position of leadership in the congregation of God's people. Whether that was an official office or simply an authority that came from their perceived wisdom is not clear. But Moses was easily able to identify these elders as natural leaders, and they were to help Moses carry the burden of the people so he would not have to do so alone.

In fact, perhaps these were men who had already been chosen from among the people. Earlier in their journey, according to Exodus 18, Moses was already becoming weary and worn out trying to serve as judge among the people, hearing and trying to mediate all their disputes. His father-in-law, Jethro, recognized that this was too much for one man to handle, and urged Moses to *"select capable men from all the people—men who fear God, trustworthy men who hate dishonest gain—and appoint them as officials over thousands, hundreds, fifties and tens."* (Exodus 18:21)

Moses did as his father-in-law suggested and chose capable men from all Israel and made them leaders of the people, officials over thousands, hundreds, fifties and tens. Perhaps these seventy men now being identified as elders were taken from this group, because they had acquitted themselves well and had become greatly respected and appreciated.

Moses was to bring them to the tent of meeting. According to Exodus 33:7-11, as the people travelled through the wilderness on the way to their Promised Land, wherever they stopped, Moses would pitch a tent outside the camp some distance away, and called it the "tent of meeting." Anyone seeking the guidance or wisdom of the LORD would go to the tent of meeting outside the camp. And whenever Moses went out to the tent, the pillar of cloud would come down and stay at the entrance, while the LORD spoke with Moses. Whenever the people saw the pillar of cloud standing at the entrance to the tent, they all stood and worshiped, each at the entrance to his tent.

It was to this tent that Moses was to bring these seventy chosen elders. God would come down and meet with them there to speak to them. *"I will come down and speak with you there."* (Numbers 11:17) They would hear the very voice of God, as He commanded and instructed them as to their duties among the people.

But even more than that, God said:

"I will take of the Spirit that is on you and put the Spirit on them." (Numbers 11:17)

This most surely was not meant to suggest that God would take away a portion of the Spirit that was on Moses, lessening His presence within Moses, to share a small measure of it with these other chosen elders. It more likely meant that some of the same gifts of wisdom and spiritual discernment God had given to Moses He would now give to these other men. They would now, like Moses, be equipped and enabled by the presence and power of the Holy Spirit within them for the functions that would be required of them as elders.

One Bible dictionary describes the work of the Spirit in the Old Testament as follows:

In the historical books, the Spirit of God empowers the leaders of Israel in various ways. That is to say, the Holy Spirit gives the leaders of Israel extraordinary authority, governmental administration, military capacity, artful craft and other abilities. These were special provisions from God that ordinary people did not receive.[13]

In other words, in the Old Testament, the Holy Spirit was not yet spread abroad among God's people, as would happen much later on the Day of

Pentecost. At this point the Spirit was given to select leaders among the people, for specific times and purposes, to enable them to function as God commanded. For example, the Spirit of God enabled the Old Testament prophets to understand the divine revelation of God's Word and communicate it to the people. The masses did not always (often) listen to the prophets or heed the Word of God, but it was the Spirit of God that empowered these prophets for the task He had given them.

When God instructed Moses in the building and furnishing of the tabernacle, He said:

> *"See, I have chosen Bezalel son of Uri, the son of Hur, of the tribe of Judah, and I have filled him with the Spirit of God, with skill, ability and knowledge in all kinds of crafts—to make artistic designs for work in gold, silver and bronze, to cut and set stones, to work in wood, and to engage in all kinds of craftsmanship."* (Exodus 31:1-5)

It was the Holy Spirit who gifted this man with the special talent to make the furnishings that were necessary. The Spirit of God was present and at work in Bezalel to assist in this great creation of God's design.

Such was to be the case here in Numbers 11. Seventy men were chosen by Moses to serve as elders, to help oversee and manage the needs of the people. And God the Father, through God the Spirit, would equip them for the task. He, the Holy Spirit, would give them the wisdom to judge correctly, lead wisely and discern clearly the needs of the people and the ways of God; just as He had done and was doing for Moses himself.

Thus we learn something about the Holy Spirit. At least part of His work was, and is, to equip, empower and enable the people of God to serve the LORD as He has appointed them so to do. It has often been said that God will not ask you to do something until and unless He first equips you to do it. He will not ask you to teach His Word—as a pastor, seminary professor, parent or church school teacher—without giving you the Spirit-led resources to do so. God will not ask you to be an evangelist calling people to faith without the Spirit of God's help to find the right times, places and words to speak God into their lives. (Please note—the people to whom you speak those saving words may not listen or respond positively. That's in the Spirit's hands as well!) God will not place you in a ministry of mercy to care for hurting people without giving you a spirit of compassion and empathy. He will equip you, through the Holy Spirit, for whatever ministry to which He calls you.

Our role is to put ourselves, through prayer and His Word, in a place where God can speak to us and guide us to His calling for us. We need to open our hearts to the Spirit, so that He can lead and equip us for the tasks at hand. Like those seventy elders had to go to the tent of meeting to receive the gift of the Spirit, we need to spiritually be open and receptive to His presence and power.

One aside: two of those seventy elect men did not go to the tent of meeting with the others. Scripture does not tell us why, but they remained in the camp and did not go out with Moses and the others. (Numbers 11:26-27) In an expression of great grace, the Spirit also rested on them where they were in the camp and they prophesied there. Nevertheless, let's agree that we will "go to the tent" in our hearts, through the disciplines of the spirit—individual and group prayer, personal and community Bible study, private and corporate worship, Christian service, fasting—to open ourselves to the Spirit's work.

It was reported that during a great mission in London, Mr. Dwight L. Moody was holding a meeting in a theater packed with a most select audience. Noblemen and noblewomen were there in large numbers, and a prominent member of the kingly family was in the royal box.

Mr. Moody stood to read the Scripture lesson. He attempted to read Luke 4:27—*"And many lepers were in Israel in the time of Eliseus the prophet."* (King James Version—Elisha in the NIV, much easier to pronounce!) When he came to the name of Eliseus he stammered and stuttered over it. He went back to the beginning of the verse and began to read again, but when he reached the name Eliseus, he could not get over it. He went back the third time, but again the word was too much for him. He closed the Bible with deep emotion and looked up and said, "Oh, God, use this stammering tongue to preach Christ crucified to these people."

The power of God's Spirit came upon him, and one who heard him then and had heard him often at other times, said that he had never heard

Mr. Moody pour out his soul in such a torrent of eloquence as he did then, and the whole audience was melted by the power of God.[14]

God's Spirit is able to take our weakness and do great things, if we are yielded to Him and obedient to His will for us. We may have stammering tongues, but God's Spirit can empower us to speak a bold witness for the truth. We may feel weak and ill at ease, but He can fill us with strength for the moment. There were many times when I ascended the pulpit to preach to my congregation when I did not *feel* ready, when my heart and spirit were not feeling inspired or empowered in the least. But often that was exactly when God took over and people were touched by the Word of the Gospel.

I heard someone say recently that God does not need much from us to do great things. After all, David only had five little stones, and he only used one! With that, God killed the giant.

As Jesus promised in Mark 13, when He was warning the apostles that they would be arrested and persecuted because of Him:

> *"Whenever you are arrested and brought to trial, do not worry beforehand about what to say. Just say whatever is given you at the time, for it is not you speaking, but the Holy Spirit." (Mark 13:11)*

We need to speak boldly for the truth. We may stand firmly for God's Word. We can testify plainly and clearly for the Gospel, in any and all circumstances, no matter how daunting. The Spirit of God will give us the right words to say and the courage to do so.

QUESTIONS FOR CONTEMPLATION OR CONVERSATION

1. Have you been a part of a congregation that was torn apart by grumbling and complaining? What happened? What role did you play in the conflict? Did you contribute to the problem or the solution? How?

2. Have you ever been so discouraged or so frustrated and defeated that you just wanted to die? Why or why not?

3. To what task, service or ministry has God called you? Do you feel capable for it? Why or why not? What would it take for you to get started?

4. Have you generally allowed the Holy Spirit to equip you for ministry? Why or why not? How could you open yourself more to Him?

5. What spiritual disciplines are most helpful to you in connecting with God the Spirit? What other ways could you try to relate to Him more closely?

CHAPTER 3

Where Can I Go From Your Spirit?

"Where can I go from Your Spirit?
Where can I flee from Your presence?
If I go up to the heavens, You are there;
if I make my bed in the depths,
You are there.
If I rise on the wings of the dawn,
if I settle on the far side of the sea,
even there Your hand will guide me,
Your right hand will hold me fast."
(Psalm 139:7-10)

We have seen the eternity of the Holy Spirit as the third Person of the Trinity. He always has been and always will be, just as God the Father and God the Son are infinite. We have contemplated His presence in our lives to empower and equip us for specific ministries to which God calls us, like He did for Moses and the seventy elders.

Now we must contemplate His *omnipresence*. God is omnipresent, and therefore the Holy Spirit is also omnipresent. It's a word that means, according to Merriam Webster: "present at all places at all times, ubiquitous, universal." The Holy Spirit of God is boundless, endless, immeasurable, infinite, limitless, unending.[15] He is not limited or restricted by time and space as are we mortal, physical beings.

As J. I. Packer said it:

"God is present in all places; we should not think of Him, however, as filling spaces, for He has no physical dimensions. It is as pure

> *spirit that He pervades all things, in a relationship of immanence that is more than we body-bound creatures can understand."*[16]

What is true of God the Father is true of God the Spirit. He is present in all places. In ways more than we can comprehend or understand, He is immanent—nearby and not far away, around us and within us (who believe in Christ) at all times and in all places. This is what David was expressing, under the inspiration of God. This is something that God has said about the Holy Spirit, the third Person of the divine Trinity.

Psalm 139 is a wonderful song that worships God in grand terms. Read it in its entirety and join your heart in David's praise. It is divided into four sections. The first, verses 1 through 6, praises God for His *omniscience*. God knows, perceives, understands and grasps everything. Nothing surprises or confounds God. There is nothing that is beyond God's wise knowledge. There is nothing God needs to learn.

It is never as if God sees some situation taking place in our life (or in the course of the nations) that surprises Him, and He says, "Wow, I never saw *that* coming! What can I do about this one?" He saw it happening long before it was ever contemplated and it was always in His predetermined plan for us from before the beginning of time. It is never that some scientist comes up with a new discovery into the workings of creation that God didn't already know, causing Him to say, "Hmm, that's interesting. I didn't know *that!*" He created it, down to the cellular level and beyond, and always knew exactly how it all would work.

God gave David the wonderful (and fearsome?) awareness that He knew when David rose in the morning and when he sat to rest. He discerned the very thoughts of David's mind and heart. He was fully aware of David's plans and pains, his fears and foibles, his works and his words. Before David could speak a single word, God already knew what it was going to be.

This knowledge was too wonderful for the king to comprehend, too "lofty" for him to understand. In the verses before our text above, David humbly exclaimed:

> *"Such knowledge is too wonderful for me,*
> *too lofty for me to attain." (Psalm 139:6)*

There are many mysteries about God and our faith that are beyond our limited capacity. At least there are for me! This was one, for David—and for me—the omniscience of God the Father, Son and Holy Spirit.

> *"He made the earth by His power;*
> *He founded the world by His wisdom*
> *and stretched out the heavens by His understanding."*
> *(Jeremiah 51:15)*

> *"For the foolishness of God is wiser than man's wisdom, and the*
> *weakness of God is stronger than man's strength."*
> *(1 Corinthians 1:25)*

> *"All this also comes from the* Lord *Almighty,*
> *wonderful in counsel and magnificent in wisdom."*
> *(Isaiah 28:29)*

What was true for David is true for us. God knows us from before we were born. As one commentator said it:

> *"Nothing about us is hidden from God. He knows when we sit down and rise up. He knows our thoughts before they ever come into our heads. He knows all about our ways. Matthew Henry says, '…He knows what rule we walk by, what end we walk towards, what company we walk with.' Furthermore, He knows every word we speak before we speak."*[17]

He knows our joys and sorrows. He sees the inmost thoughts and desires of our hearts. He is aware of our plans for the future, and yet knows already how things will all work out for us. God has His own plans for us, and His agenda for us may very well be different from our own. Guess which will prevail! God is omniscient. That can be both comforting and unsettling.

It's good to know that God is aware of our every heartache and sorrow. There is great comfort in that. He already knows how He is going to strengthen us, see us through and work for our good in everything. We can trust His wisdom in our afflictions. There is great comfort and encouragement in that awareness.

But God also knows those "secret" angers, judgments and unkind thoughts. We can hide nothing from Him because He is omniscient. So when I hit my thumb with the hammer and let out some words I would be embarrassed for others to know I have uttered, God hears it. When that car cuts me off on the highway and I inwardly wish the driver some ill will, God knows it. When I look enviously at my friend's fancy, expensive new car, then think of my thirteen-year-old almost-antique, and covet their wealth and good fortune, God knows. When someone says or does something to hurt, demean or disrespect me, and bitter resentment enters my heart, God sees it there. Nothing is hidden from Him. That staggering truth could (and rightfully should) be reason for pause and some deep repentance.

The second segment of the song, verses 7 through 12, celebrates God's *omnipresence*, specifically in reference to the Holy Spirit. So in Psalm 139, God the Father again speaks of God the Spirit and tells us that the Spirit is everywhere present, all the time. We'll come back to this one in a moment.

First, to finish our brief overview of the Psalm, the third stanza, verses 13-16, is a celebration of God's *omnipotence*. God can do anything. God is almighty. God is powerful beyond description. There is nothing God cannot do. God created David in his inmost being and knitted him together in his mother's womb. No child is an "accident." Every child who was ever born was carefully created by God, to be exactly what God designed for them to be. Each and every human child is lovingly planned, purposefully created and carefully knitted together by God's mighty hand.

Nothing is impossible to God, as Jesus ably showed. Heal the sick, still the raging storm, cast out demons, feed the thousands with a few crumbs, restore the dead to life and walk on water: it was all within the range of His omnipotence. God's power and might is infinite.

Take that even further, God is powerful enough to move peoples and nations to do His bidding. Mighty world leaders believe that their power is ultimate. It is not. God's is. Unbeknownst to them, God is moving behind the scenes to accomplish His purposes for His creation. Everything lives and moves at His discretion, and nothing is done that is beyond His ability to use according to His desires.

As the Lord said to Abram, when He promised a child to him and Sarah in their old age (they were well beyond child-bearing age by normal, human terms):

> *"Why did Sarah laugh and say, 'Will I really have a child, now that I am old?' Is anything too hard for the L*ORD*?" (Genesis 18:13-14)*

That was a rhetorical question. The answer, of course, was no. When Job humbly (finally) bowed before the LORD's overpowering questioning and wisdom, he said:

> *"I know that You can do all things;*
> *no plan of Yours can be thwarted.*
> *You asked, 'Who is this that obscures My counsel*
> *without knowledge?'*
> *Surely I spoke of things I did not understand,*
> *things too wonderful for me to know." (Job 42:2-3)*

Many, many other Scripture passages celebrate the power and might of God.

> *"Lift your eyes and look to the heavens:*
> *Who created all these?*
> *He who brings out the starry host one by one,*
> *and calls them each by name.*
> *Because of His great power and mighty strength,*
> *not one of them is missing." (Isaiah 40:26)*

> *Jesus looked at them and said, "With man this is impossible, but with God all things are possible." (Matthew 19:26)*

And the final strophe, verses 17-24, expresses David's deep awe and praise, his plea for God's help against his enemies, and his prayer to be known fully and intimately by God. This is a natural and necessary response to a God so glorious and great. He deserves our reverence and deepest praise.

But now back to the text printed above. This is an expression of God the Spirit's omnipresence. *"Where can I go from Your Spirit? Where can I flee from Your presence?"* (Psalm 139:7) God, and specifically God the Spirit, is everywhere. There is nowhere He is not. David tried to think of someplace where he could go to escape from the Spirit's presence. Could I get away from Him in the highest heaven? No, He is surely there. Could I flee to the very depths of Sheol? No, He is even there. The King James Version says it more graphically:

> *"If I ascend up into heaven, Thou art there:*
> *If I make my bed in hell, behold, Thou art there!"*
> *(Psalm 139:8, KJV)*

Could I fly with the light of the dawn sun, to the farthest side of the largest sea? Even there, the Spirit of the living God would already be.

I think naturally of the Old Testament prophet Jonah, he of the big fish. Jonah was called by God to take the word of grace to the foreign city of Nineveh. Jonah did want not to go. Nineveh was the capital of his nation's most hated enemy. Jonah had no desire to go to such a dangerous and wicked place. And he certainly had no wish for them to hear the Word of God and be saved. That was the last thing Jonah would have wanted. He would have much preferred that they would face the judgment and wrath of God.

I tremble to admit that I fully understand how he must have felt. In my weaker moments, there are peoples (Al Queda or ISIS terrorists?) and nations (Iran, Iraq, current Afghanistan?) I'm sad to admit, that I'm not sure I would even want to hear (and much less respond) to the Gospel. In fact, I relish the thought that some will one day receive their just "reward" for the evil they have committed in this life.

All of which vainly and self-righteously ignores the stark truth that I deserve God's wrath as much, if not infinitely more, than they do, and that it is only by the immeasurable grace of God that I myself have any hope for my own redemption.

But that's how Jonah felt, I assume. So he boarded a ship and headed for Tarshish, in the opposite direction, foolishly thinking to escape God and avoid His calling. But He could escape God's presence no more than could David. A huge storm arose on the sea, the sailors discerned that somehow Jonah was the cause of it and, at Jonah's insistence, they threw him overboard. A huge fish (many think of it as a whale, but the Bible does not specify) swallowed him and carried him for three days in its belly, after which Jonah repented of his foolish disobedience to God. The big fish vomited Jonah out onto dry land, and God repeated His command to Jonah.

This time, he obeyed. No surprise there. Jonah tried to flee from the presence of God and failed. There was no place he could go to escape the presence of the Spirit of God.

> *"The heavens, even the highest heaven, can not contain You."*
> *(1 Kings 8:27)*

> *"'Am I only a God nearby,' declares the L*ORD*,*
> *'and not a God far away?*
> *Can anyone hide in secret places*
> *so that I cannot see him?' declares the L*ORD*.*
> *'Do not I fill heaven and earth?' declares the L*ORD*."*
> *(Jeremiah 23:23–24)*

> *"The God who made the world and everything in it is the Lord of heaven and earth and does not live in temples built by hands."*
> *(Acts 17:24)*

All of the above assure us that wherever we are, God the Spirit is. He is present everywhere. We sometimes imagine that God is present in His temple, in the buildings we call churches—"God's house" we call it—as if He lived there. We feel a special sense of sacred awe when we go there, and perhaps we should. Those are places that are set apart for the very special purpose of celebrating and praising the one true God. But then we may be tempted to think (like Jonah?) that He is not "out there," wherever we go when we exit those doors.

But as God said above, He is both nearby and far away, filling heaven and earth. Even the highest heaven cannot contain Him. There are no secret places for us to hide where He cannot see us. *"Where can I go from Your Spirit? Where can I flee from Your presence?"* Nowhere!

An interesting side note here: It's true that God the Spirit is everywhere present and there is nowhere He is not. But we may not always recognize that presence or be aware of Him so near to us. In Genesis 27 and 28, we read the story of Jacob deceiving his father, Isaac, and receiving from him the blessing that was rightfully his brother Esau's. When Esau learned of the deception, he threatened revenge. So Jacob fled to his uncle, Laban, in a distant land.

On the way, he had a dream in which he saw a stairway resting on the earth with its top reaching to heaven, and the angels of God were ascending and descending on it. God Himself came to him in this dream and promised to continue the covenant that He had made with his grandfather, Abraham, and his father, Isaac, pledging to make him (Jacob) into a great nation, with countless descendants and a rich land to call their own, all in the distant future.

When the dream had ended, Jacob said:

"Surely the LORD is in this place, and I was not aware of it."
(Genesis 28:16)

Jacob was almost overwhelmed with a sense of the presence of God. The sacred had intruded in his journey and he was suddenly aware that something extraordinary had happened; Someone divine had intervened. That awareness was unique to him, and intensely powerful. As one commentator has said, "His language and his conduct were like that of a man whose mind was pervaded by sentiments of solemn awe, of fervent piety and lively gratitude."[18]

The point is that God the Spirit was *always* near and around Jacob, but Jacob simply was not spiritually perceptive or mature enough to sense it.

I wonder how many times in my life or yours was God present to us in His Spirit and we did not even recognize Him? Do we live our daily lives in the full awareness of His constant presence? Or do we merrily go our way, totally oblivious to the omnipresent Spirit of God? Do we experience the nearness of the Spirit as an occasional happenstance that occurs only in specific times of spiritual retreat, emotional worship or deep insight into some spiritual truth?

Certainly He is present to us in such moments of high inspiration. But are those the only times He manifests Himself to us? Is He not also there by our side (actually, *within* us if we are believers in Christ) every other moment of our lives? As we have seen, David realized that he could never escape the presence of the Spirit. Jonah learned the same thing. Jacob realized that the Spirit of the LORD was present to him even before he was aware of it.

Whether we "feel" it or not, whether we can sense His presence or are totally unmindful of Him, He is there. What J. I. Packer said about God the Father is true also of God the Spirit:

> *"One thing that is clear, however, is that He is present everywhere in the fullness of all that He is and all the powers that He has, and needy souls praying to Him anywhere in the world receive the same fullness of His undivided attention…He is able to give His entire attention to millions of individuals at the same time."*[19]

What a comforting assurance that is! Wherever we are, wherever we go, whatever we face, God the Spirit is there with us. "*Whithersoever thou turnest thyself, thou wilt see God meeting thee.*"[20] He is there for us in countless ways: with a welcomed sense of God's love; in a deep experience of joy; to explain and illuminate the Scriptures as we read them; giving comfort and peace in times of sorrow or fear; to grant spiritual gifts for ministry and service; to empower us to boldly speak the Word of God into someone's life; and much more.

The Spirit Himself may be invisible to our *physical* senses, but for those with *spiritual* eyes to see, His power and presence are clearly all around us.[21] May God grant us the perception and awareness to know that He is there for us, and to trust in that comforting, guiding and empowering Spirit.

QUESTIONS FOR CONTEMPLATION OR CONVERSATION

1. In what ways is knowing that the Holy Spirit is omnipresent (everywhere present) a comfort to you? Why?

2. In what ways is knowing that the Holy Spirit is omnipresent a fearsome or disturbing reality to you? Why?

3. In what situations are you most aware of the Spirit's presence in your life? What have been some of the places/circumstances when you most felt His nearness?

4. In what situations are you least aware of the Spirit's presence in your life? What is it that makes you doubt His nearness? Why?

5. What could you do to cultivate a deeper sensitivity to the Holy Spirit?

CHAPTER 4

A New Spirit in You

"'For I will take you out of the nations; I will gather you from all the countries and bring you back into your own land. I will sprinkle clean water on you, and you will be clean; I will cleanse you from all your impurities and from all your idols. I will give you a new heart and put a new spirit in you; I will remove from you your heart of stone and give you a heart of flesh. And I will put My Spirit in you and move you to follow My decrees and be careful to keep My laws.'" (Ezekiel 36:24-27)

We come now to a most encouraging word from God about the Holy Spirit. It is found in the writings of the prophet Ezekiel. In the year 606 B.C., the Babylonians began the first of several deportations of the Jews; Daniel was in this group. In the second group (597 B.C.) was a young man named Ezekiel. Five years after Ezekiel was taken to Babylon, he was called to be a prophet of God. So while another prophet, Jeremiah, was ministering to the people back home, Ezekiel was preaching to the Jews who were in captivity in Babylon.[22]

Ezekiel's prophetic words from God told of His coming judgment on Jerusalem (chapters 4-24); then of God's judgment on the surrounding nations for their cruelty to God's chosen people (chapters 25-32); and finally ended on the hopeful note of God's restoration of His people (chapters 33-48). Our text above comes from that latter section of Ezekiel's Old Testament book, and thus is part of the promise of God's gracious renewal of the kingdom.

After so many oracles of judgment and condemnation on the people and priests of Israel for their unfaithful idolatry, God made it clear that His purposes in electing the Hebrews to be His chosen people would not be frustrated, even by their own disobedience. He would continue to fulfill His promises and plans through the faithful remnant. God's story was not at an end. There was much more to come.

In Ezekiel, we find a remarkable promise of the coming Messiah, Jesus:

> *"I will place over them one shepherd, My servant David, and He will tend them; He will tend them and be their shepherd. I the LORD will be their God, and My servant David will be prince among them. I the LORD have spoken." (Ezekiel 34:23-24)*

This is not literally speaking about David, who had lived many centuries *prior* to Ezekiel, but of One *like* David, the coming Messiah. Jesus would be the true, Good Shepherd, and would one day rule in righteousness and peace. So the promise of restoration clearly includes the reign of God the Son, Jesus.

But in our text above, we read a different kind of promise from God, no less remarkable, concerning God the Spirit. The people of God had been conquered, deported and scattered among the nations of the world. At various times, and from the operation of diverse causes, the Jews were separated and scattered into foreign countries *"to the most distant land under the heavens"* (Deuteronomy 30:4).

Many were dispersed over Assyria, Media, Babylonia, and Persia, descendants of those who had been transported thither by the Exile. The ten tribes of Israel, after existing as a separate kingdom for two hundred and fifty-five years, were carried captive (721 B.C.) by Shalmaneser (or Sargon), king of Assyria. They never returned to their own land as a distinct people, although many individuals from among these tribes, there can be no doubt, joined with the bands that returned from Babylon on the proclamation of Cyrus.[23]

To these scattered, dispersed people, God promised through Ezekiel a glorious restoration and reconciliation:

> *"'For I will take you out of the nations; I will gather you from all the countries and bring you back into your own land." (Ezekiel 36:24)*

One day these people of God would be allowed to return to their homeland. The nation of wanderers and exiles would be reunited and restored as a unity.

But it would not come immediately, and it would not be in the manner they might have expected. Centuries later, Jesus' brother James would pen his New Testament letter addressing it to *"the twelve tribes scattered among the nations."* So even then, that portion of God's promise had not yet occurred. Not until the twentieth century would the people of Israel return to the Promised Land as an independent, self-governing nation. God's timing is far different from what we might expect!

Another part of His promise, however, is even more germane to our topic here.

> *"I will sprinkle clean water on you, and you will be clean; I will cleanse you from all your impurities and from all your idols." (Ezekiel 36:25)*

It was their own idolatry and disobedience that had led to their exile. Because of their sin God had allowed them to be taken captive and dispersed to the ends of the earth.

But now God was promising to cleanse them from all of their impurities and sin. God Himself would wash them and provide for their purification. How would He do this? It would be only through the blood of the promised Messiah shed on the cross for our atonement. As the apostle Paul said it:

> *"And that is what some of you were. But you were washed, you were sanctified, you were justified in the name of the Lord Jesus Christ and by the Spirit of our God." (1 Corinthians 6:11)*

The apostle John agreed:

> *"But if we walk in the light, as He is in the light, we have fellowship with one another, and the blood of Jesus, His Son, purifies us from all sin." (1 John 1:7)*

The cleansing and purification from sin that God promised is available in only one way—by trusting in what Christ has done on the cross to pay the penalty we deserve. We have no righteousness of our own. Our lives do not merit or earn God's favor, no matter how good and exemplary we may think them to be. We can never be pure enough to deserve God's mercy. It is only through Jesus Christ that we can be cleansed and forgiven.

> *"Salvation is found in no one else, for there is no other name under heaven given to men by which we must be saved." (Acts 4:12)*

Some time ago a traveling evangelist was singing to himself the song, "I've Been Redeemed." A fellow passenger, hearing, joined him in the song. After singing, the evangelist put the question to the stranger, "Have you been redeemed?" "Yes, praise the Lord," was the answer. "May I ask how long since?" "About nineteen hundred years ago," he replied.

The comment was astonishing and the evangelist began to think his new friend was a bit eccentric or peculiar. "Nineteen hundred years ago?" "Yes, sir, but I'm sorry to say it's not much more than a year that I have known it."[24] He was referring, of course, to what Christ did on the cross, now nearly two thousand years ago, shedding His blood to pay the penalty for our sin and offering salvation and forgiveness to all who would believe. That was when all true believers were ultimately saved. That was the cleansing God had promised through Ezekiel all those centuries ago.

Not only that, for those who do truly believe, it was God Himself who enabled them to do so. How did I come to believe the Gospel of salvation by faith in Christ? How did you? It was only by the regenerating work of God's Spirit within us. We did not do it by virtue of our own wisdom or great perception. We did not deduce the truth through our own superior ability to reason things through. We did not figure it out in our own minds. No, it was none of the above.

Like everyone else we were totally dead in our sins, unable to even *want* to turn to God.

> *"As for you, you were dead in your transgressions and sins, in which you used to live when you followed the ways of this world and of*

> *the ruler of the kingdom of the air, the spirit who is now at work in those who are disobedient." (Ephesians 2:1-2)*

We were God's enemies, separated from Him by a vast chasm, and unable to even desire to cross it. People who are dead cannot make themselves alive again. They need something or someone from outside themselves to make it happen.

As Dr. D. Martyn Lloyd-Jones said it:

> *"The natural man can do nothing, he is utterly helpless, spiritually dead. What makes us Christians? He hath 'quickened us.' He has done it by His power, the power of the Spirit. What brings us into salvation is that the Spirit of God begins to work in us and to act upon us, to convict us of sin, to open our eyes. He does it all—'by grace ye are saved'."[25]*

So we are all dead in our sin and unable to desire or to choose for ourselves to come alive. We need Someone from the outside to come along and raise us to spiritual life and make us able to choose to believe. That is exactly what God promised through Ezekiel.

> *"I will remove from you your heart of stone and give you a heart of flesh. And I will put My Spirit in you and move you to follow My decrees and be careful to keep My laws." (Ezekiel 36:25-27)*

"I will replace your heart of stone," God said. "I will put My own Spirit in you and move you to turn to Me." It is the Holy Spirit who enters our hearts and makes us alive to God, enabling us to choose to believe the Gospel and begin to live for Christ. When Jesus promised the coming of the Spirit, He said, *"When He comes, He will convict the world of guilt in regard to sin and righteousness and judgment."* (John 16:8) It is the conviction of the Holy Spirit that enables us to perceive and acknowledge our sin, and to understand and respond to the Gospel. He is the new, living Spirit that God grants to all who are chosen to be His. Only through the

Holy Spirit's prior, initiating work in us can we be saved. As Paul said it to the Thessalonians:

> *"For we know, brothers loved by God, that He has chosen you, because our gospel came to you not simply with words, but also with power, with the Holy Spirit and with deep conviction." (1 Thessalonians 1:4-5)*

It is all only by the grace of God. As the great Reformers said it: *Sola Gratia, Sola Fide, Sola Christos;* only by grace, only through faith, only in Christ. It is only by the grace of God that the Holy Spirit convicts, awakens and enables us. Even to trust in Christ comes from God, and by trusting Christ we become children of God. As far back as the ancient days of Ezekiel, God promised to make that happen.

The Welsh poet and pastor, George Herbert, 1593-1633, said it this way:

> *Then will I trust, said I, in Him alone,*
> *Nay, ev'n to trust in Him, was also His;*
> *We must confesse, that nothing is our own.*
> *Then I confess that He my succor is.*[26]

Even to trust in God comes from God. Nothing is our own. This is a remarkable promise from God concerning the Holy Spirit that should move us to utter humility and awe. Who are we that God should care for us? Who are we that God should do this for us, miserable sinners that we are? Why should God move in our hearts to awaken our souls to Him and enable us to trust in Christ?

Copernicus was a great mathematician. His studies and calculations revolutionized the thinking of mankind about the universe. When he lay dying, *The Revolution of the Heavenly Body* was placed in his hands. It had just been printed. At death's door, he saw himself, not as a great scholar, or an astronomer, but only as a sinner in need of the Savior.

On the tombstone at his grave at Frauenberg are carved the following words which he himself chose for his epitaph: "I do not seek a kindness equal to that given to Paul. Nor do I ask the grace granted to Peter. But that forgiveness which Thou didst grant to the robber—that, earnestly I crave!"[27] This was a man who knew that his only hope for eternity lie within the mercy of God, as provided on the cross of Jesus Christ.

This raises two questions in my mind. I'm sure there are more, but only two that I will consider here. First, if no one comes to faith apart from the initiating work of the Holy Spirit within, why does God not do such work in *everyone*? Clearly not everyone on earth comes to a saving faith in the atonement offered by Christ. This must mean that God's Spirit did not enable them to do so. Why did the Holy Spirit awaken *my* dead soul, and not my neighbor's?

As Jesus said it:

"All that the Father gives Me <u>will come to Me</u>, and whoever comes to Me I will never drive away." (John 6:37, emphasis mine)

Or, as God the Father said it through the prophet Isaiah:

"So is My word that goes out from My mouth:
It will not return to Me empty,
but will accomplish what I desire
and achieve the purpose for which I sent it." (Isaiah 55:11)

This assures us that all whom God has chosen (predestined) will come to Jesus, and Jesus will not cast them aside. God's Word will achieve the purpose for which He sent it; it will not be ultimately resisted or rejected.

All of which means that if you are a true, believing Christian, if you have put aside your own feeble attempt to earn God's favor by your own will and ways, and have trusted in Christ alone for your eternal salvation, it is because—and only because—God chose you and sent the Holy Spirit to awaken your heart and soul to Him, enabling you to believe.

"You did not choose Me, but I chose you and appointed you to go and bear fruit—fruit that will last." (John 15:16)

"But we ought always to thank God for you, brothers loved by the Lord, because from the beginning God chose you to be saved through the sanctifying work of the Spirit and through belief in the truth." (2 Thessalonians 2:13)

This is reason for great humility and inexpressible gratitude. Not because of anything I have done or could do, O Lord, only by Your mercy. As all the angels, elders and living creatures surrounding the throne of God in heaven fall down on their faces before Him in worship, so must we.

"Amen!
Praise and glory
and wisdom and thanks and honor
and power and strength
be to our God for ever and ever.
Amen!" (Revelation 7:11-12)

This is our motivation for regular worship attendance. This compels us to make thanksgiving a regular and major component of our daily prayers and devotion.

Are we grateful people? To be a Christian without deep gratitude to God is a contradiction in terms. An old farmer visited a large city. In a restaurant before eating, the man bowed his head in a prayer of thanksgiving. Seeing this, a young man seated nearby sneeringly asked, "Say, old man, back where you come from does everyone pray before he eats?" The farmer quietly replied, "The hogs don't."[28] A bit pointed, perhaps, but could it be said that a Christian without proper gratitude is on the level of an animal?

The Gospel of Luke tells us of ten men with leprosy who came to Jesus, begging for help. Jesus sent them away to show themselves to the priests for ritual cleansing. They dutifully obeyed. On the way, all ten found that they had been healed. One of the ten came back, praising God and throwing himself at Jesus feet to give thanks. Jesus asked,

"Were not all ten cleansed? Where are the other nine? Was no one found to return and give praise to God except this foreigner?" Then

> *He said to him, "Rise and go; your faith has made you well."*
> *(Luke 17:18-19)*

May we always be like that one, and never like the nine. May we always return to Jesus, in worship and praise, falling at His feet in grateful humility.

One commentator reminds us of the old adage which suggests that counting sheep will help you go to sleep. He suggests that for the Christian, it would be better to count God's blessings. "You cannot exhaust that number. But reflecting on His blessings will bring joy to your heart and drive out worry. Then you will know God's peace—and so, to sleep!"[29]

> *"Speak to one another with psalms, hymns and spiritual songs. Sing and make music in your heart to the Lord, always giving thanks to God the Father for everything, in the name of our Lord Jesus Christ." (Ephesians 5:19-20)*

May we be people who sing and make music in our hearts to God, always giving thanks to God, the Father, Son and Holy Spirit.

A second question in this regard that is often raised is this: If we are saved only if and when God so enables our faith by the work of His Holy Spirit, then what of our free will? Some hold that we are capable, by our own free will, to choose to accept God's offer of grace or to, on the other hand, reject it. The final determining factor is our free choice.

The more Biblical position, I believe, is that we cannot accept God's gift of salvation unless He chooses us for it and regenerates us by His Holy Spirit, enabling us to accept. First God gives life to our dead spirits, *then* He enables us to have faith. It is not the other way around.

How all of this fits together with our free will is beyond my pay grade. The Bible affirms that we have been given free will, and we are responsible for our use of it and the very real choices we make, including our choice to believe or not believe the Gospel. At the same time, the Bible also clearly affirms the complete sovereignty of God even over those choices we make. It also states that it is only by the grace of God that we can be saved, not by anything we do or are capable of doing in our own right.

Theologians use the word "compatibilism" to describe how God's sovereignty is compatible with human freedom and our moral responsibility. As Scott Christensen states it:

There is a dual explanation for every choice humans make. God determines human choices, yet every person freely makes his or her own choice. God's causal power is exercised so that He never coerces people to choose as they do, yet they always choose according to His sovereign plan.[30]

Theologians may understand all that, but to me it's a paradox, or a mystery, which I am at a loss to explain. You will have to study this further at the feet of teachers much more wise and learned than I.

In the end, all I can say is that we will indeed be held accountable for our ultimate, personal choice for or against Christ, and that if we have chosen to believe and trust in Him as our Savior and Lord, then we should bow in humble thanks for the grace of God in choosing us for salvation and for the work of the Holy Spirit to make it a reality.

QUESTIONS FOR CONTEMPLATION OR CONVERSATION

1. What promises from God are you still waiting to be fulfilled? How does it make you feel to have to continue to anticipate the coming promise?

2. What words would you use to describe your heart and life before you came to the true faith? Dead? Separated from God? Lost? Enemy of God? Other:

3. How does it make you feel to contemplate God's grace in choosing you for redemption?

4. Would you consider yourself a person of gratitude and humility? Why or why not?

5. What do you do on a regular basis to show your gratitude to God for your salvation? What more could you do this week to express your thanks to Him?

6. How do you understand the interplay between human free will and the election/regeneration/salvation from God? How can both be true?

CHAPTER 5

I Will Pour Out My Spirit

> *"And afterward, I will pour out My Spirit on all people. Your sons and daughters will prophesy, your old men will dream dreams, your young men will see visions. Even on My servants, both men and women, I will pour out My Spirit in those days."*
> *(Joel 2:28-29)*

After wandering in the wilderness for forty years, God's people were on the verge of finally entering their "Promised Land." The generation that had disobeyed and refused to trust God had mostly passed away, and a new generation was poised to take hold of the ancient covenantal promises given to Abraham, Isaac and Jacob. They had already become a numerous people, as God had promised. Now was the time to enter the land God had also appointed for them, from before the Exodus itself.

> *"So I have come down to rescue them from the hand of the Egyptians and to bring them up out of that land into a good and spacious land, a land flowing with milk and honey—the home of the Canaanites, Hittites, Amorites, Perizzites, Hivites and Jebusites."*
> *(Exodus 3:8)*

But Moses, who would not enter the land with them because of his own sin (see Numbers 20), first wanted to remind the people of all that God had done for them up to this point, and to sternly charge them to obey the Law that God had given them. It was in essence a renewal of the covenant, celebrating the gracious blessings of God upon these people, and recalling their responsibilities as God's chosen nation to live in holiness and obedience.

In Deuteronomy 28, Moses rehearsed the blessing that would be theirs if they faithfully obeyed the commands of God: peace and protection against all their enemies, fruitful harvests in all the land, productive flocks and herds, bountiful food supplies, abundant prosperity, a healthy and multiplying people. God would grant them blessings beyond description, and make them the greatest nation on earth, a witness to the holy name of God.

> *"The LORD will make you the head, not the tail. If you pay attention to the commands of the LORD your God that I give you this day and carefully follow them, you will always be at the top, never at the bottom. Do not turn aside from any of the commands I give you today, to the right or to the left, following other gods and serving them." (Deuteronomy 28:13-14)*

BUT—if they should *fail* to obey God, if they were *not* faithful to Him, dire consequences would follow. They would be cursed by God. Their crops would fail, they would face devastation, drought, famine, plagues and diseases, and defeat at the hands of their enemies. Deuteronomy 28:15-68 contains a long and fearsome list of the pestilence and destruction they would experience as God's judgment for their lack of faith and purity before God.

One specific potential punishment was reminiscent of one of the ten plagues God sent upon the Egyptians to force them to free the Israelites from slavery: locusts. If they were to turn from following the one true God—

> *"Swarms of locusts will take over all your trees and the crops of your land." (Deuteronomy 28:42)*

Yahweh God, speaking through His prophet Moses, warned the people that one consequence (among many) of their disobedience would be swarms of locusts that would devastate their crops and devour the fruit of their fields.

Now jump ahead in time, from the day of Moses (circa 1400 B.C.) to the day of the prophet Joel (unknown with any certainty but perhaps somewhere around 500 B.C.). In the centuries after Moses renewed the covenant between God and His people, much had happened. The people had indeed disobeyed God and been faithless to Him, countless times. They never seemed to maintain their trust in Him or their exclusive devotion to Him. The people, their leaders and even their priests were always chasing after false idols and turning away from the God who had chosen and freed them, just as He knew all along they would.

To be sure, there is and always has been only one true God. There have been countless *false* gods and goddesses, all arising from the imaginations of people's hearts, but none have had any reality or substance. They have been pure inventions and imaginings of people determined to turn away from God Himself to one of their own liking. But turn the people did.

As a result, in the intervening years they had faced numerous judgments and chastisements from God. Some of these judgments drove them back to God, some did not. And even if they did return to Him, it was always a temporary spiritual awakening that quickly faded back into idolatry. Interestingly, the specific punishment God mentioned in Deuteronomy 28 through the prophet Moses, came to pass in the days of the prophet Joel. A plague of locusts, in numbers that defied description, devastated the land.

Locusts were a common problem in the ancient Near East. The destruction they caused was infamous. A locust can consume its own weight every day, and swarms were known to cover as many as four hundred square miles. Even one square mile can hold over one hundred million locusts.[31] This is the kind of pestilence being described by the prophet Joel:

> *"What the locust swarm has left*
> *the great locusts have eaten;*
> *what the great locusts have left*
> *the young locusts have eaten;*
> *what the young locusts have left*
> *other locusts have eaten."* (Joel 1:4)

By the time this great swarm had moved on, there was nothing left of their crops and fields. Besides that terrible swarm of hungry insects, however, a terrible drought immediately followed. Inevitably, horrible famine was the result. There was nothing left of their crops, trees or foliage. No grain, no fruit of the vine, nothing was left alive. It was like nothing they had ever seen before. *"Has anything like this ever happened in your days or in the days of your forefathers?"* (Joel 1:2) It was a plague of historic proportions.

The prophet Joel's message came in the midst of this national tragedy. But it was not just a natural catastrophe, to Joel. He saw in the invasion of the locusts the hand of God. Joel told the people that God was disciplining them for their foolish disobedience and idolatry. This present disaster and famine was the direct result of their own sin.

However, Joel saw even something else. "Joel used the immediate condemnation of God (the locusts) as an illustration of a future, ultimate judgment, 'the day of the LORD'."[32] Joel speaks often about the coming great and terrible day of the Lord. According to some eschatological views, "the day of the Lord" is that future time, described in Revelation 6-9, when God will "rapture" the church, taking true believers to heaven, and pour out His wrath on the unbelieving world during the great tribulation. It will all end with the Battle of Armageddon (Joel 3:9–17; Revelation 19:11–21), and with Jesus Christ returning to the earth to establish His kingdom.[33]

Other "End Times" viewpoints put a different order to such things, and perceive the culmination of history and the second coming of Christ in varying ways. But God spoke through Joel about wonders in heaven and on earth, blood and fire and billows of smoke. The sun will be darkened and the moon turned to blood, all occurring before the coming *"of the great and dreadful day of the LORD."* (Joel 2:31) It will be a cataclysmic, terrible and chaotic time in the heavens and on earth, and God's wrath will be complete.

In the midst of that terrible judgment of God, there will be deliverance for all who call on the name of the LORD. God assured us through Joel that those whom God has called and chosen, and who have truly trusted in His grace through Christ, will be saved. And not only that, something quite remarkable will occur. God will "pour out [His] Spirit on all people." (Joel 2:28)

I Will Pour Out My Spirit

"And afterward, I will pour out My Spirit on all people. Your sons and daughters will prophesy, your old men will dream dreams, your young men will see visions. Even on My servants, both men and women, I will pour out My Spirit in those days." (Joel 2:28-29)

As we noted earlier (in chapter 2), in Old Testament days the Holy Spirit of God was given to select leaders among the people, for specific times and purposes, to enable them to function as God commanded. Moses was given the Spirit of God to enable him to lead the people to freedom. King Saul was given the Spirit of God to reign over the people—temporarily, at least—until God removed His Spirit from Saul in response to his disobedience. The Old Testament judges, many of them, and the prophets as well, were given the Spirit of God to speak His word and His warnings to the people. All were specific fillings of the Holy Spirit for particular times and reasons.

"Afterward," after the Day of the Lord, the Holy Spirit would be poured out in a much broader way. To pour out implies an abundant, complete, overflowing amount. One commentator uses the phrase "extravagant to the point of unnecessary."[34] The gift of the indwelling Holy Spirit will no longer be limited to a select few, for a restricted time and for a narrowly defined purpose. God will pour out the Spirit in the most expansive way imaginable, and all His people will be blessed.

We should not take the phrase *"on all people"* (Joel 2:28) literally. It has been suggested, rather, that it means all of God's elect, of all races and nationalities.[35] That seems a reasonable interpretation to me, and one I will assume here. Rather than being limited to specific people, after the Day of the Lord, God will broadly pour out His Spirit on all true believers. Men, women, sons and daughters, people of all races and ethnicities, will dream godly dreams and see Spirit-inspired visions. In the first sense, Joel was speaking to the people of Judah. But in eschatological terms of the Day of the Lord, it refers to Jews as well as Gentiles of all the nations on earth.

We also saw in chapter 2 how Moses selected seventy elders from among the people, and God placed His Spirit upon them for their service to the people. Two of those elders, named Eldad and Medad, had remained in the camp. They were listed among the elders, but did not go out to the tent with Moses and the others. Yet the Spirit also rested on them, and they prophesied in the camp. Joshua, Moses' aide and protégé, spoke up and urged Moses to stop them. But Moses replied,

> "Are you jealous for my sake? I wish that all the LORD's people were prophets and that the LORD would put His Spirit on them!" (Numbers 11:29).

Joel predicted the day when Moses would see his wish fulfilled.

It *was* fulfilled—at least *partially*—on the day of Pentecost. In Acts chapter 2, the believers were all together in one place, when suddenly a sound like the blowing of a violent wind came from heaven and filled the whole house where they were sitting. They saw what seemed to be tongues of fire that separated and came to rest on each of them. *All of them* were filled with the Holy Spirit and began to speak in other tongues as the Spirit enabled them. (Acts 2:1-12) People from all over the world, speaking different languages, all heard the Gospel in their own tongues. It was an amazing event; and the apostle Peter, in explaining what was happening, said, *"This is what was spoken by the prophet Joel."* (Acts 2:16)

Ever since then, whenever anyone who has been chosen by God is regenerated, granted the gift of faith, puts their trust in Christ as Savior and Lord, and is forgiven of their sins, the Spirit of God enters in and takes up residence in their hearts. Every true believer has the Holy Spirit within.

> "'Whoever believes in Me, as the Scripture has said, streams of living water will flow from within him.' By this He meant the Spirit, whom those who believed in Him were later to receive." (John 7:38-39)

> "And I will ask the Father, and He will give you another Counselor to be with you forever—the Spirit of truth. The world cannot accept Him, because it neither sees Him nor knows Him. But you know Him, for He lives with you and will be in you." (John 14:16-17)

He comes to teach us all things and remind us of everything Jesus has said to us (John 14:26); to guide us into all truth (John 16:13); and to empower us in our witness to the Gospel (Acts 1:8). We will consider such things in later chapters.

It is the Holy Spirit Who enables us to testify to the truth and to share the Gospel with others. It is the Holy Spirit Who takes our weak and hesitating testimony and uses it to convince the hearer of their sin, guilt and coming judgment. It is the Holy Spirit Who enables them to respond to that witness with repentance and faith, just like He did for us (John 16:8-11). When God broadly poured out His Holy Spirit, He made possible the awakening of faith in millions of people all across the world—of all races and nationalities.

But believers being *indwelt* by the Spirit (since the day of Pentecost) is very different from being *filled* with the Spirit. *"Afterward,"* after the great and terrible Day of the LORD, whatever that means and however that occurs, the Holy Spirit will be poured out in an even deeper, fuller way on all those who are true believers, filling them to the utmost. "This will be true regardless of age, gender, or social class."[36] All will be truly Spirit-*filled* people, living by the power, guidance and inspiration of God the Holy Spirit. All will dream dreams and see visions. All will prophesy and speak the Word of the Living God.

Think of someone you know whom you perceive to be a mature, saved believer; someone who seems to you to be a spiritual, Spirit-filled Christian with a life of loving obedience and faithfulness to Jesus, deeply connected to and abiding in Him. Please know that appearances can be deceiving, and even the best Christians have their own problems, weaknesses, sins and trials. None of us is perfect or has obtained holiness yet—nor will we until God Himself completes His work in us in our glorification. See Paul's words in Philippians 3.

But think of someone whom you consider to be much further along the path than you see yourself to be. Now kick that up a few notches and try to imagine someone who is <u>fully</u> indwelt by the Holy Spirit and living in intimate, personal communion with Him. Even that may not be the full picture of what will come through God's Spirit after that time.

The text says that *"Your sons and daughters will prophesy, your old men will dream dreams, your young men will see visions."* (Joel 2:28) Dreams, visions and prophetic words are all gifts of the Holy Spirit. This may simply mean that everyone will be gifted in some special and profound way for the furtherance of the Gospel and the work of God's Kingdom. "Prophesying in the New Testament is applied to all speaking under the enlightenment of the Holy Spirit, and not merely to foretelling events."[37] We will all be enabled to speak boldly and effectively for Christ through the Holy Spirit's power.

How amazing it will be to hear millions of Christians proclaiming the saving grace of God in Christ more effectively than the best evangelists the world has ever seen to date. How incredible it will be to hear countless believers teaching God's Word with more ardor and clarity than the most helpful theologians and Bible instructors in history. Imagine the constant, ardent and fervent worship of innumerable Spirit-filled saints the world over, raising hearts and voices in praise to God. All this will happen when the Spirit of God is poured out broadly upon His people.

I read of someone who said in a sermon that if the Holy Spirit was suddenly taken out of this world, ninety-five percent of what we are doing in our churches would continue without pause, as if nothing had happened.[38] That's because so much of what we do, even in faithful, evangelical churches, is totally disconnected from the Holy Spirit of God. Imagine what will be accomplished for the Gospel when God so broadly pours out His Spirit in the Day of the Lord!

Imagine what *we* might accomplish even today for the Kingdom of God if we submitted more fully to the Spirit's power and control. Maybe I am speaking only for myself—but I think probably not—when I say that I have depended upon God's Spirit to indwell me and help me through this life of hardship and toil, but I have not *wholly* submitted to Him and allowed Him to fill me to the maximum. Imagine the impact we could have on this present world if we yielded ourselves fully to the Holy Spirit!

Dwight L. Moody once illustrated this truth as follows: "Tell me," he said to his audience, "how can I get the air out of this glass?" One man said, "Suck it out with a pump." Moody replied, "That would create a vacuum and shatter the glass." After many impossible suggestions, Moody smiled, picked up a pitcher of water, and filled the glass. "There," he said, "all the air is now removed." He then went on to show that victory in the Christian life is not by "sucking out a sin here and there," but rather by being filled with the Spirit.[39]

Are you *filled* with the Holy Spirit of God? Am I? No, and none of us truly will be until that time when we are glorified by God in His eternal presence; or as spoken here by Joel, after that time, after the return of Christ in power and sovereign majesty. Until then, may we seek to open ourselves more and more to Him, and may we yield more and more to His presence and power working in and through us.

Over the years I often illustrated this by referring to an electric lamp. It works well, and provides great light to scatter the darkness—as long as it is plugged into the electrical outlet in the wall. Without a connection to the source of electricity, that lamp is useless. Just so, unless we are connected to and relying upon our source of power for life, the Holy Spirit, we are likewise defeated and feeble.

QUESTIONS FOR CONTEMPLATION OR CONVERSATION

1. What word(s) would you use to describe the presence of the Holy Spirit in your life? Why?

2. How has God gifted you to contribute to the work of the Gospel?

3. To whom or what do you normally turn for encouragement, instruction, empowerment or enablement in your life of faith? Why?

4. As you think about what it means to be truly filled by the Holy Spirit, what are your thoughts and feelings about the coming event?

5. What could you do to yield yourself to the Spirit more fully today?

CHAPTER 6

By My Spirit

"So He said to me, 'This is the word of the LORD to Zerubbabel: 'Not by might nor by power, but by My Spirit,' says the LORD Almighty.'" (Zechariah 4:6)

In B.C. 586 the Babylonians destroyed the city of Jerusalem and the temple, and took the people captive. In B.C. 539, Babylon fell to Cyrus II, a Persian king whose military victories eventually put him in possession of the largest empire the world had yet seen. The conquests of Cryus II began with Media (549), followed by Lydia (546) and then Babylonia (539).[40]

Cyrus was a somewhat benevolent ruler who treated his conquered people with tolerance and equanimity. Accordingly, he permitted a remnant of the Jews to return to their homeland, to be sure as vassals of his sovereign reign. In 535 they laid the foundation for the rebuilding of the temple. But the work stopped due to fierce opposition and discouragement, and it was not until 520 that the Jews again began to restore God's house.

Zechariah, son of Berechiah, was a young man who came from a long and respected line of priests and prophets. His very name meant *"the LORD remembers,"* and God did indeed remember His promises to His people. In fact, Zechariah's father's name meant *"the LORD blesses,"* and his grandfather's name meant *"His time."* Put them all together, as Warren Wiersbe suggested, and you have *"the LORD remembers to bless in His time."*[41]

God remembered to bless in His own divine timing, and He spoke through an angel to Zechariah (and his contemporary, Haggai) to encourage the people and give hope for the future, sometime around 500 B.C. Through a series of eight visions, God spoke of His anger at the nations for what they did to His people and to His holy city, His future plans to bless and restore Israel, to cleanse them from their sin, to reinstate them as a priestly nation and even of the coming Messiah:

> *"Rejoice greatly, O Daughter of Zion!*
> *Shout, Daughter of Jerusalem!*
> *See, your king comes to you,*
> *righteous and having salvation,*
> *gentle and riding on a donkey,*
> *on a colt, the foal of a donkey."* (Zechariah 9:9)

Does that sound familiar? That's a passage we often hear read on Palm Sunday, as we celebrate the arrival of Jesus into Jerusalem, in fulfillment of Zechariah's prophecy. God kept that very promise in full detail!

The quote at the outset of this chapter, Zechariah 4:6, comes from the fifth of those eight God-given prophetic visions, and it concerns a golden candlestick and two olive trees. The candlestick, or lampstand, had seven lamps, each connected with seven pipes that led upward to a bowl. The bowl was connected to two olive trees, one on the left and one on the right, from which it received a continuous supply of oil to keep the light burning.

The identity of the two olive trees can be debated, but many see them as representations of Zerubbabel, the governor of Judah, and Joshua, the high priest at that time. This is not the Joshua of Genesis fame, the revered successor to Moses and conqueror of Canaan, but a priest by the same name centuries later. So you have the priestly and the kingly roles expressed here. The angel said:

> *"These are the two who are anointed to serve the Lord of all the earth."* (Zechariah 4:14)

The lampstand itself is often understood to denote the nation of Israel, standing as a light to the nations; and the bowl of oil is said to symbolize the abundant supply of power from God the Holy Spirit to enable their witness to the one true, triune God. And this is exactly what we are told about God the Spirit—*His* is the power for our service to the King, and that

His power is more than sufficient for whatever He calls us to perform for the good of His Kingdom.

Zerubbabel was the political leader whose task it was to organize, fund and oversee the rebuilding of the temple that the Babylonians had so thoroughly destroyed. There was vehement opposition to that great project, as it could be said there is to *any* project of divine origin. Satan, our enemy, is always seeking to oppose and defy anything God does.

The nation of Judah, and the city of Jerusalem, was in a greatly weakened state. The surrounding nations looked on them with scorn and derision. Some were afraid that if the city were to embark on a rebuilding program, even if only the temple, those nations would think that Judah was trying to reassert its political and military strength, and would quickly move to crush them. Indeed, those nations were rattling their sabers and making threats to that effect. Therefore many Jews fearfully sought to impede and even prevent the project altogether.

Others had seen the plans for the new temple, which was a significantly scaled back version of the original that David had prepared for and Solomon had constructed. It was to be a smaller, less ornate, less imposing structure, which would have been understandable given the rather downtrodden political, social and financial state of affairs in Judah at that time. But some, who remembered the glory of Solomon's temple, were embarrassed, and they too worked to hinder progress.

So Zerubbabel was facing some stiff opposition from within and from beyond the city limits of Jerusalem. It was a daunting task for any political leader of a demoralized and oppressed nation. He may well have faced the task with great fear and trepidation. So God spoke a word directly to the governor, through the prophet Zechariah, by way of the angel:

> *"'Not by might nor by power, but by My Spirit,' says the* L<small>ORD</small> *Almighty." (Zechariah 4:6)*

This is our word from God the Father about God the Holy Spirit. It is by the *Spirit's* power that the work of God will be accomplished. It is the Holy Spirit Who will empower, enable, energize and endow the work God calls forth from His people. The rebuilding of the temple, in an earthly, human sense, was in the hands of the governor. But ultimately and definitively it would be accomplished only by the power of the Holy Spirit working through Zerubbabel and all the others who supported and were involved in the project. It was not by Zerubbabel's managerial skills, not by his political leadership, or his ability to inspire confidence in his subjects—it would be by the power of the Spirit of God.

Many years before this, God chose the Hebrew people to be His own, not because of their great numbers, power or might. They were a small, insignificant band of slaves at the time. God chose them not because of what *they* would do for Him, but for what *He* planned to do through and for them. It was to be done by the power of God.

When those same people faced the fearsome prospect of conquering the populations inhabiting the land promised to them by God, He assured them:

> *"Do not be terrified by them, for the LORD your God, Who is among you, is a great and awesome God." (Deuteronomy 7:21).*

It was to be done by the power of God.

When the king of Aram went to war against Israel, he surrounded the city of Dothan, where the Israeli prophet Elisha was staying, in an attempt to capture him and keep him from speaking God's words of warning and guidance to the king of Israel. When Elisha and his servant awoke one morning and looked out over the city wall, they saw horses and chariots surrounding the city. The servant panicked and said, "Oh, my lord, what shall we do?" And Elisha said,

> *"Don't be afraid … Those who are with us are more than those who are with them." (2 Kings 6:16)*

And when God opened the eyes of the servant to see the spiritual realities, he saw the hills full of horses and chariots of fire, all around the enemy. And the victory was ultimately won—by the power of God.

In Judges 3 we read how the Israelites did evil in the eyes of the LORD; forgetting the LORD their God by worshiping and serving false gods. In His just wrath, God allowed them to become subject to the king of Aram Naharaim, who oppressed them for eight years. *"But when they cried out to the LORD, He raised up for them a deliverer, Othniel son of Kenaz, Caleb's younger brother, who saved them. <u>The Spirit of the LORD came upon him</u>, so that he became Israel's judge and went to war."* (Judges 3:7-11, emphasis mine) The LORD gave the king of Aram Naharaim into the hands of Othniel, who overpowered him. So the land had peace for forty years.

In Judges 6 and 7, God chose Gideon to lead his people in battle against the Midianites. To say the least, Gideon was not the most self-assured warrior God could have chosen. After much fearful hesitation, Gideon agreed. But when he gathered an army to go into battle against their oppressors, God said, *"You have too many men for Me to deliver Midian into [your] hands. In order that Israel may not boast against Me that her own strength has saved her."* (Judges 7:2)

So God directed Gideon to whittle down the army until he was left with only three hundred men of war, to go into battle against the thousands of their enemy. The victory was then won decidedly and undeniably by the power of God.

In the Gospel of Mark, in response to the rich young man who turned away from following Jesus rather than surrender his wealth, Jesus said, *"How hard it is for the rich to enter the kingdom of God! ...Children, how hard it is to enter the kingdom of God! It is easier for a camel to go through the eye of a needle than for a rich man to enter the kingdom of God."* (Mark 10:23-25)

The disciples were amazed, and despaired of anyone ever being saved from God's just wrath. In their view, people of great wealth were blessed by God because of their goodness and faithfulness, and were obviously favored by God as a result. Sounds a lot like today's health and wealth teaching, doesn't it?

Jesus looked at them and said:

"With man this is impossible, but not with God; all things are possible with God." (Mark 10:27)

Salvation—for all who are truly saved—is by the power of God. His Spirit convicts, convinces, regenerates and enables our faith (John 16:7-14). With the Spirit of God even this is possible, for the wealthy and for the poor. All things are possible with God.

When Napoleon, a man of small physical stature, started to fight England and Austria, the soldiers called him "Wee One Hundred Thousand Men." They would ask one another during battles, "Is Wee One Hundred Thousand Men in the army today?" His genius and leadership were worth that many soldiers in their minds. [42]

If <u>God</u> be for us, who can be against us? Inspired and empowered by the Spirit of God, we can do all things. As the apostle Paul said it:

> *"I know what it is to be in need, and I know what it is to have plenty. I have learned the secret of being content in any and every situation, whether well fed or hungry, whether living in plenty or in want. I can do everything through Him who gives me strength." (Philippians 4:12-13)*

What we learn from God's word through Zechariah to Zerubbabel is that it is by the Spirit of God, not through our own power or might, that we can do all things. Apart from Him we can do nothing of eternal value (John 15:5). As an unnamed poet said it:

> *"Without Me ye can do nothing."*
> *Lord, I know, I know!*
> *"Without Me ye can do nothing"—*
> *Only a round "O."*
> *Stand by my side, O Master,*
> *Then One and O are ten;*
> *Stand by my friend and me, Lord—*
> *We are a hundred then.*
> *A little group of two or three*
> *Are gathered in Thy name—*
> *'Tis a hundred or a thousand if*
> *Thou'rt standing there with them.* [43]

This is something every believer needs to keep in mind on a daily basis. As the world around us continues to spiral out of control, as violence proliferates, as the chaos in our cities grows and multiplies, as our beloved Lord Jesus is increasingly mocked and blatantly disregarded, His church ever more marginalized, and His followers more and more openly and fiercely persecuted, we need to rely on the power of the Spirit to enable us to stand firm in our faith.

We cannot and will not be able to do it by our own strength and might. We simply do not have the personal, inner resources to stand up to the forces arrayed against us. As one author reported:

> A tide was kept back strangely for twelve hours once, and so a host of Christians in Holland were saved from slaughter by the Duke of Alva. A tremendous wind once scattered the Armada of Spain over the wastes of the North Sea, and so Protestant England was spared to the world. John Knox moved his usual seat away from before the window one night, pressed by a feeling he could neither understand nor resist; an hour later there came a musket-ball crashing through the glass and burying itself harmlessly in the opposite wall. Thus has God interposed and protected his children.[44]

I entered ministry as a young man woefully unprepared and inadequately trained theologically and Biblically. The large part of the reason for that, of course, was my own fault for not taking my classes and lessons seriously enough. But also contributing to the insufficiency of my seminary education was the fact that I attended a liberal school where few of the professors would have reasonably been considered evangelical or conservative. Some did not even believe in the inerrancy of Scripture or the sufficiency of Christ for our salvation. I spent years reading, studying on my own and attending continuing education seminars to make up for what was lacking in my Biblical and theological understanding.

And yet, in spite of my inadequacies, we were blessed to see God accomplish many things over the years in and through our ministry. People were brought to a saving faith. Others were encouraged to deepen their walk with God and to grow in their own Biblical obedience. Ministries of outreach impacted the communities around us in sometimes remarkable ways.

How was any of that even possible? It was certainly not through the power and might of a badly trained and spiritually immature pastor such as myself. It was not by the force of will of the people in my congregations. It was only by the grace and power of God the Holy Spirit that anything at all was accomplished, as He chose to work and move in our midst.

Dr. D. Martyn Lloyd-Jones said it this way:

> "This power of the Lord is not only round and about us, and not only caring for us and planning for us, but it is in us. 'The exceeding greatness of His power to us-ward that believe.' ... Remember the energy and the power that is working in us, and remember that it is invincible because it is His. Let the devil and all his powers come, we can 'Stand in His great might, with all His strength endued'."[45]

It is often pointed out, and rightly so, that after Jesus' crucifixion, His disciples were frightened, defeated and cowering behind closed doors. They had deserted Jesus and were hiding in fear for their own lives. It was an unimpressive, motley crew, to say the least.

And yet, they would in short order become amazingly bold and fervent, fearlessly proclaiming the risen Christ openly, in public, traveling the known world, facing down religious and political authorities who sought to silence them, and courageously enduring unspeakable punishments and persecutions for the name of their (and our) Lord. What happened to transform them so?

It was the power of the Holy Spirit, Who entered into them on Pentecost day (Acts 2:1-13), energizing and enabling them to unflinchingly withstand any and all pressures, harassments, tortures and torments to tell others about the saving grace of God in Christ. Not through their own personal strength, but by the power of God through the Holy Spirit. And the world was changed by this handful of formerly fearful and shrinking men and women.

It was Peter, himself arrested, imprisoned and flogged for the cause of the Gospel, who said:

"Dear friends, do not be surprised at the painful trial you are suffering, as though something strange were happening to you. But rejoice that you participate in the sufferings of Christ, so that you may be overjoyed when His glory is revealed. If you are insulted because of the name of Christ, you are blessed, for the Spirit of glory and of God rests on you." (1 Peter 4:12-14)

It was the *"Spirit of glory and of God"*—the Holy Spirit—which rested upon Peter and the others and enabled them to stand tall for Christ. Read through Hebrews 11 sometime, looking at the hardships and persecutions people endured, and the great things they accomplished for God. How did they do all that? It was by their faith, yes, in one sense. But from where did that faith come? It was by the power of God the Spirit in them. They did not stand by their own strength; if so they would have failed miserably, one and all. Everything that is celebrated in Hebrews 11 was the result of the grace and glory of God.

Think back over your own life. How many times have you overcome great hardship and even oppression? How many times have you had to stand up publicly and be counted for Christ against the tide of public harassment? How many times have you tackled some kind of ministry in the body of Christ's church, knowing full well you had neither the ability nor resources to do it, and yet God used you to accomplish great things for His glory? How many times have you faced persecution, embarrassment or mockery for the sake of the Gospel?

How were you able to do so? It was not by your own inner fortitude and courage, that much is certain. It was only by the grace and glory of God working in and through you.

Have we never faced such affliction for the cause of Christ? Perhaps that is because we have lived in a nation where our faith has been—at least in years past—tolerated and even respected. That is no longer the case. Our faith is being increasingly attacked, marginalized and denied in our culture, and open persecution has already begun.

How will we endure such intolerance and even attack? If you seek to stand by your own inner resources in these coming days you are in deep weeds, to use a golf image with which I am intimately familiar. When I golf,

I spend an inordinate amount of time hunting for my lost golf ball in deep weeds and in dark, verdant forests, when I am supposed to be out on the sunny, manicured fairway. In other words, left to our own resources, we are in trouble.

What other types of challenges are you facing, aside from persecution and intolerance? Are there financial struggles in your life, not knowing how to "make ends meet," or even from where your next meal is coming? Do you have the heartache of broken relationships that you long to reconcile, but you just can't seem to make that happen? Are there trials of physical illness, injury or incapacitation? Countless other life hurdles could come to mind—fill in the blank. Are you trying to overcome or solve them by your own strength?

We need to turn to God, opening ourselves to and relying upon the grace and the power of His Holy Spirit. *"'Not by might nor by power, but by My Spirit,' says the LORD Almighty."*

QUESTIONS FOR CONTEMPLATION OR CONVERSATION

1. What have been some of the extremely difficult situations or circumstances you have faced in your life? How have you most often attempted to deal with them?

2. Do you tend to turn to God as your first source of help and hope in times of trouble, or do you turn to Him only after your own resources have failed? Why?

3. When you do accomplish something of note, personally or for the Kingdom, to whom do you tend to give praise and credit? Why?

4. What could you do to more quickly turn to and to more fully submit to the power of God's Spirit within?

5. How have you experienced the empowerment of the Holy Spirit in your life up to this point? How could that encourage you going forward?

CHAPTER 7

A Spirit of Grace and Supplication

"And I will pour out on the house of David and the inhabitants of Jerusalem a Spirit of grace and supplication. They will look on Me, the One they have pierced, and they will mourn for Him as one mourns for an only child, and grieve bitterly for Him as one grieves for a firstborn son." (Zechariah 12:10)

Zechariah was a common name in Biblical days, given to at least thirty men in the Old Testament. He was: one of the chiefs of the tribe of Reuben (1 Chronicles 5:7); one of the porters of the tabernacle (1 Chronicles 9:21); a Levite who assisted at the bringing up of the ark from the house of Obededom (1 Chronicles 15:20-24); one who assisted in teaching the law to the people in the time of Jehoshaphat (2 Chronicles 17:7); one of the "rulers of the house of God" (2 Chronicles 35:8); and a chief of the people in the time of Ezra, who consulted him about the return from captivity (Ezra 8:16).[46] He was also the son of Jeroboam, who followed his father and became king of Israel in Samaria, reigning for only six months and doing great evil in the eyes of the Lord (2 Kings 15:8-9).

So when we speak of Zechariah, we must be careful to distinguish exactly to which Zechariah we are referring. In this case we are speaking of Zechariah the prophet and author of the next to the last book of the Old Testament. (See the beginning of the preceding chapter of this book for more of his history.) The text above is a small portion of the oracles given through him by the Lord God Almighty to encourage His people—both in exile and those back in the homeland.

In this particular prophecy, God promised that He would use the nation of Judah to send His judgment and wrath on the nations of the world.

> *"I am going to make Jerusalem a cup that sends all the surrounding peoples reeling. Judah will be besieged as well as Jerusalem. On that day, when all the nations of the earth are gathered against her, I will make Jerusalem an immovable rock for all the nations. All who try to move it will injure themselves. On that day I will strike every horse with panic and its rider with madness, declares the LORD. I will keep a watchful eye over the house of Judah, but I will blind all the horses of the nations. Then the leaders of Judah will say in their hearts, 'The people of Jerusalem are strong, because the LORD Almighty is their God'." (Zechariah 12:2-5).*

The day is coming, God assured His people, when the LORD's Messiah will come to this earth, and the Kingdom of the LORD will be established. The Day of the LORD is coming, the nations will rise up to fight against it, but the LORD Himself will go out to defeat them and place His King over all nations and peoples. *"The LORD will be King over the whole earth. On that day there will be one LORD, and His name the only name."* (Zechariah 14:9)

The Messiah, Jesus, has already come—once—about two thousand years ago. At that time, He was resisted, rejected, denied and accused. Ultimately, though innocent and sinless, He was put to death on a cross to pay the just penalty for the sins of all who would believe and trust in Him. He rose from the dead and ascended to heaven, to sit at the right hand of the Father. In that sense, the Kingdom of God has already been established. But it has not been consummated.

However, one day, perhaps very soon, He will *return* in power and judgment over the nations of earth, and the unbelieving powers of earth and the godless nations will fall before Him. At that time, God's Kingdom will be fully accomplished. We who are His by reason of our faith look forward to His return and the fullness of His reign with great anticipation and joy.

The bad news is that there will be some very harsh, dreadful days ahead for us as human history draws to a close and before He comes to consummate His kingdom. We may be seeing the beginnings of those "end-times" (as they are often called) even as we speak. But the good news is that it will all conclude with the return of Christ in glory and His ultimate victory over the enemies of God. All of His chosen and saved followers will share with Him in that final glory.

At that time, God promised through Zechariah to pour out His Spirit *"on the house of David and the inhabitants of Jerusalem."* As one commentator described it:

> Jerusalem, following the awful days of the end-time, shall be re-peopled and replenished, but it will not be until Christ returning in glory is recognized by Israel as He whom they have pierced. He will put down all enemies and work a gracious work in His people.[47]

When Christ returns at the end of days, the Chosen People, Israel, will finally, en masse, recognize Him as Messiah. Currently they do not, as a whole. Yes, there are some "Messianic Jews" who have accepted Jesus as their Savior, but the nation, in its entirety, has not. But when Jesus returns in power and glory, their eyes and hearts will be opened, and they will fall down before Him as Messiah.

They will understand what was done to Him the first time around: He was tortured, mocked and crucified by those who refused to believe His Word and to receive His Gospel of salvation by faith. But when He comes the second time, it will all become very, very clear. He was the One they were waiting for all along! The injustice and agony He endured for us will then be undeniable. And they will mourn with deep distress for what was done to Him, the *"One they have pierced."*

> *"They will look on Me, the One they have pierced, and they will mourn for Him as one mourns for an only child, and grieve bitterly for Him as one grieves for a firstborn son. On that day the weeping in Jerusalem will be great, like the weeping of Hadad Rimmon in the plain of Megiddo. The land will mourn, each clan by itself, with their wives by themselves: the clan of the house of David and their wives, the clan of the house of Nathan and their wives, the clan of the house of Levi and their wives, the clan of Shimei and their wives, and all the rest of the clans and their wives." (Zechariah 12:10-14)*

In the ancient day when this word was first given through God's prophet, to be without a child among God's people was considered a curse and a great shame. Notice Elkanah an Ephraimite, recorded in 1 Samuel 1. He had two wives; one was called Hannah and the other Peninnah. Peninnah had children, but Hannah had none. Peninnah regularly mocked and provoked Hannah, so Hannah wept and refused to eat because of her barrenness. It was considered a terrible thing for a woman to have no children. That will be the weeping and wailing of God's people at the return of Christ: as a woman with no children.

As we might imagine, what was even worse was to have a son and then to lose him—to illness, warfare or any other such tragic cause. Think of Exodus 12, which describes the last and most horrible plague used by God to free His people from slavery in Egypt. After all the previous plagues had failed to move Pharaoh to free the Hebrews—the water turned to blood, the frogs, the gnats, the flies, the killing of the livestock, the boils, the hail, the locusts and the darkness—the Lord struck down the firstborn of Egypt:

> *"At midnight the L*ORD *struck down all the firstborn in Egypt, from the firstborn of Pharaoh, who sat on the throne, to the firstborn of the prisoner, who was in the dungeon, and the firstborn of all the livestock as well. Pharaoh and all his officials and all the Egyptians got up during the night, and there was loud wailing in Egypt, for there was not a house without someone dead." (Exodus 12:29-30)*

Can we even imagine the bitterness of the mourning that took place in Egypt on that day of God's wrath? The weeping and wailing must have been unspeakable because of the overwhelming losses that were experienced throughout the kingdom: the firstborn of the royal family and officials, the firstborn of the people of the nation, the firstborn of the prisoners in the jails, even the firstborn of the livestock! They all suffered the pain of loss. Such will be the weeping and wailing of God's people at the return of Christ.

The mention of Hadad-rimmon is also revealing. Hadad-rimmon was a place or city in the great plain of Esdraelon. It was the battlefield of many a conflict, near Megiddo. There was much lament and mourning for warriors lost in all those confrontations and wars. In fact, this odious site was the likely scene of the death of King Josiah in battle with Pharaoh-necho of Egypt. King Josiah was one of the few godly rulers in Judah, whose reign was a rare bright spot in the nation's later history. His death was deeply mourned, and the prophet Jeremiah wrote lamentations for the occasion (2 Kings 23:29, 30; 2 Chronicles 35:22–27).[48]

> *"Jeremiah composed laments for Josiah, and to this day all the men and women singers commemorate Josiah in the laments. These became a tradition in Israel and are written in the Laments." (2 Chronicles 35:25).*

The great mourning of God's people, as thus described by Zechariah, will be the result of their regret for the injustices done to Christ at His first incarnation, and also in repentance for their own sin and complicity. Prior to His "Second Coming," many will this time bow before Christ and receive Him as Savior, and there will be a great spiritual awakening among the people of God. As some scholars believe, this refers to the Jewish nation *and* those around the globe who have previously not believed in Christ. Even among the believing Jews and Gentiles, God will work His wonders in those latter days preceding the return of Christ as King.

As part of that great divine movement in the hearts of God's people, the LORD promised:

> *"And I will pour out on the house of David and the inhabitants of Jerusalem a Spirit of grace and supplication." (Zechariah 12:10)*

This is God's promise of the Holy Spirit being poured out on the house of David and the inhabitants of Jerusalem, on all Israel and beyond.

In those dramatic days the Holy Spirit of God will be poured out and produce in people a "gracious disposition, and inclination for supplications."[49] We could talk here first of all about the amazing grace of God Himself, being poured into the hearts of His elect to enable them to finally believe in Christ as Messiah and to fully accept the salvation He offers to those who do so. It is only by the grace of God and the regeneration of our hearts by the Holy Spirit that we are able to believe and be saved. I would suggest that this merciful work of God is at least part of what is being referred to here.

Another part of it could very well be, as John Calvin suggests, that the Holy Spirit of God will implant and foster within those who believe at least some measure of the same grace and mercy God mercifully showed to them. In Hebrew, "grace" and "supplications" are kindred terms; so we could translate this as "gracious supplications." The plural there implies *constant* prayers, "praying continually," as Paul urged in 1 Thessalonians 5:17.

Imagine a world peopled by millions of believers who seek to love and serve Christ, and who are filled with a sense of the mercy of God towards those around them, and who are continually on their knees in prayer for the church, the world and those around them! What a remarkable scene to envision! How different will the world be as a result!

Our world today is one of ideological conflict, racial discord and political controversy. It is now a "cancel-culture," where those who do not submit to prevailing sensitivities and beliefs are attacked, criticized, vilified, blocked from social media and some have even lost their jobs. It seems like every day I read reports of people who were fired and ostracized for simply saying or writing something that is considered "misinformation" by a certain powerful portion of our society, even when it may indeed be very true.

Speakers who are scheduled at conferences or colleges are protested and un-invited for holding to positions that just a short time ago were considered mainstream. Professors are terminated for refusing to agree to and teach certain radical theories and philosophies, or to refer to students with their chosen pronoun, even when it is contrary to their physical, biological gender. Small business owners are sued into oblivion for not cooperating with practices that contradict their personal faith beliefs, such as refusing to make cakes or provide flowers for ceremonies that go against their long and firmly held convictions.

I have often remarked that even the good old fashioned character quality of courtesy is diminishing exponentially. Many people—certainly not all, but many—no longer hold doors for those coming along behind them or thank those who do so for them, treat their elders with respect, etc. Too many are so self-immersed and self-centered that they give little thought to the feelings of others. Just look at the aggressive, determined way many people drive their cars and you get a sense of the deteriorating spirit of our contemporary culture.

In a poll a few years ago, eighty-nine percent of those questioned said that incivility is a serious problem, while only one percent believed their *own* behavior to be uncivil.[50] That's interesting. Perhaps I need to contemplate my own behavior more honestly, even as I bemoan that of the people around me. Clearly it is easier to see a lack of courtesy in others than it is to see it in yourself.

Now imagine the day to come when the Holy Spirit of God is poured out on millions of His chosen people, filling them with a character molded after that of God Himself: merciful, gracious, kind, long-suffering and loving. Imagine the power of all those people praying constantly, seeking the will, ways and kingdom of God to come onto this earth as it is in heaven. What a remarkable impact that will have on the state of affairs around this globe.

Dwight L. Moody once described his own experience of the grace of God being poured into his heart:

> One day in New York—what a day! I can't describe it! I seldom refer to it! It is almost too sacred to name! I can only say God revealed Himself to me! I had such an experience of love that I had to ask Him to stay His hand! ... I would not be back where I was before that blessed experience.[51]

Now think about millions of people around the world simultaneously experiencing a similar movement of the love and grace of God in their hearts. Can we even imagine the impact of such a spiritual awakening as that? It will be earth changing, to say the least.

Civility, at least among and from God's people would be the norm, not the exception. Even those who do not accept God through Christ will be able to see the difference and will notice the kindness and courtesy they receive from others, setting an example they might even follow themselves. Maybe even things would calm down on our highways!

All this would be because people have experienced in a profound way the grace and mercy of God's Spirit in their own hearts, and have begun to share the same with those around them. The *Arizona Republic* once reported:

> As Terry Mikel was speeding toward Tucson, he passed a car—an unmarked Arizona Highway Patrol car. The officer pulled Terry over. When Terry explained that he was late for a class he was teaching at the University of Arizona, the officer

took pity on him and let him off with a warning. Before he went back to the patrol car he said, "Slow down and drive safe."

Mr. Mikel, an English professor, felt obligated to correct him. "Excuse me, Sir, it should be 'Slow down and drive safely.' You said 'Drive safe'." The officer walked back to his car and wrote him a $72 speeding ticket.

He would have been better served to return the grace he had been given!

What a glorious day it will be when the Holy Spirit is poured out on countless people of God to give them a spirit of grace and supplication, and when millions of us will begin to express that spirit more clearly in our interactions with others, and people will see the love and mercy of God reflected in us. Can that fail to draw others into the Kingdom?

The late theologian, Carl Michalson, used to tell of returning home with his wife from a night out and being greeted at the door by the babysitter who, when she saw them, dissolved into tears. It seems that she had dropped a radio and broken it. Michalson said that in one sense he was glad to see that she cried, because they'd had some babysitters who would have blamed it on the children, or would have patched it up so that when the next person used it, the radio would fall apart.

But in another sense, he said, they were deeply saddened by her tears. He wrote this, "To think that she did not know we are the kind of people who had the grace to assimilate that kind of thing." They were sad to know that their reflection of God's love did not assure this young girl that they would treat her with understanding and mercy.

It makes me wonder if my own personal grace and kindness adequately reflect the love of God to those around me. Do they see God's reflection in my character and personality? Would they intuitively know that they would receive patience, forgiveness and mercy from me, or would they expect something quite different? I want them to see Jesus in me, but would they?

One day, perhaps soon, because of the outpouring of the Holy Spirit, which God has promised through the prophet Zechariah, the love, mercy, grace and kindness of God will be clearly lived by His people, and it will be a bright witness for Christ and His Gospel. One day, people will be drawn to us, and through us to the Savior. What a great day that will be!

QUESTIONS FOR CONTEMPLATION OR CONVERSATION

1. Are you ready for the difficult days just prior to the return of Messiah, Jesus? If not, why not? What could you do to better prepare?

2. What words would you use to describe the current culture around us? Is your perception of it generally positive or negative? Why?

3. Have you ever been convicted of sin, and felt remorse so deep that it caused you to literally weep and mourn? What was that like for you? How did you deal with it?

4. Can people clearly see the grace and love of God in your life by how you treat others around you? What could you do to better reflect His love?

5. Is your prayer life one of continual supplication, or occasional outpouring because of need? What could you do to widen and deepen your prayer life?

CHAPTER 8

The Spirit of Your Father

"Be on your guard against men; they will hand you over to the local councils and flog you in their synagogues. On My account you will be brought before governors and kings as witnesses to them and to the Gentiles. But when they arrest you, do not worry about what to say or how to say it. At that time you will be given what to say, for it will not be you speaking, but the Spirit of your Father speaking through you." (Matthew 10:17-20)

Early in His earthly ministry, Jesus gathered His twelve chosen disciples and gave them authority to cast out demons and heal every disease. They were: Simon (who is called Peter) and his brother Andrew; James son of Zebedee, and his brother John; Philip and Bartholomew; Thomas and Matthew the tax collector; James son of Alphaeus, and Thaddaeus; Simon the Zealot and Judas Iscariot, who betrayed Him (Matthew 10:2-4).

Then He sent them out for an apparently short time to preach the coming of the Kingdom of God, while He travelled alone into Galilee to preach in the towns there (Matthew 11:1). Christ's commission to these twelve men for this somewhat preliminary ministry was only to minister among the people of Israel, not to the Gentiles and not even to the Samaritans. They were to announce the coming of the kingdom just as John the Baptist and Jesus Himself had done.[52]

Jesus gave them detailed instructions to guide them on the way, recorded in Matthew 10. He told them what to take for the journey; where to go—and not to go; and where to stay—and not to stay.

> *"Do not go among the Gentiles or enter any town of the Samaritans. Go rather to the lost sheep of Israel. As you go, preach this message: 'The kingdom of heaven is near.' Heal the sick, raise the dead, cleanse those who have leprosy, drive out demons. Freely you have received, freely give. Do not take along any gold or silver or copper in your belts; take no bag for the journey, or extra tunic, or sandals or a staff; for the worker is worth his keep." (Matthew 10:5-10)*

He even instructed them how to respond to those who would receive or listen to them, and to those who would not:

> *"As you enter the home, give it your greeting. If the home is deserving, let your peace rest on it; if it is not, let your peace return to you. If anyone will not welcome you or listen to your words, shake the dust off your feet when you leave that home or town." (Matthew 10:12-14)*

Some of the directives Jesus shared with them had much broader applications than to that immediate ministry. In fact, there are some who think that Jesus, beginning at Matthew 10:16, actually transitioned from speaking about the current situation they were facing to speak about things they would encounter in the years to come. He may even very well have been speaking to believers down through the ages, with an eye to persecutions to be faced as the end of time approaches, during the period now known as the Great Tribulation, just prior to the return of Christ.

So while the guidance given to the disciples in Matthew 10:1-15 may have had a more direct function for that specific day and time, and relates to us only by way of general principles, the later word in verses 16 and following most likely speak more explicitly to us today, who live in those very "end times."

And a central theme of Jesus' words of instruction and comfort for those later days deal with the persecutions to come. Here and elsewhere (Matthew 5:11, Matthew 23:34-35, Matthew 24:8-10, Luke 21:12-19, John 16:1-2) Jesus made it clear that His followers would have to contend with a culture that was disbelieving, to say the least; antagonistic to put it more bluntly. As Jesus

Himself was harassed, tormented, mistreated and tortured, so Jesus assured us would all who seek to follow and serve Him in the coming ages.

> *"A student is not above his teacher, nor a servant above his master. It is enough for the student to be like his teacher, and the servant like his master. If the head of the house has been called Beelzebub, how much more the members of his household!" (Matthew 10:24-25)*

> *"If the world hates you, keep in mind that it hated Me first. If you belonged to the world, it would love you as its own. As it is, you do not belong to the world, but I have chosen you out of the world. That is why the world hates you. Remember the words I spoke to you: 'No servant is greater than his master.' If they persecuted Me, they will persecute you also." (John 15:18-20)*

Jesus warned us of very hard days to come. We will be hated for our faithfulness to Christ. We will be persecuted and driven from city to city. We will be arrested and prosecuted by the authorities above us, religious as well as civil. Even family and friends will rise up against us in those days. Christ and His church will be opposed at every turn and on every level. Much of this seems to me to be happening even as we speak. Christ's return may be near indeed!

In spite of the dangers and distresses, those days of tribulation will also be a time of great opportunity. We will have multiple openings to shine forth the love and grace of God in how we care for those who are hurting and reach out to those who are lost. And we will be given opportunities to speak up for the truth and for the Christ we serve.

> *"Be on your guard against men; they will hand you over to the local councils and flog you in their synagogues. On My account you will be brought before governors and kings as witnesses to them and to the Gentiles." (Matthew 10:17-18)*

Notice that even while persecuted and prosecuted, we will have opportunity to witness for Christ. Even on trial, we will be able to voice a testimony for the Lord and to make Him known even in the courts of law.

I think of Peter and John, in Acts 4, being arrested and put on trial for "teaching the people and proclaiming in Jesus the resurrection of the dead" (Acts 4:2). They were jailed and then brought before the religious rulers, elders and priests. While being interrogated, Peter preached Christ to them and gave his iconic proclamation:

> *"Salvation is found in no one else, for there is no other name under heaven given to men by which we must be saved." (Acts 4:12)*

He and John were threatened and ordered not to speak or teach in the name of Jesus ever again. But, of course, they did and the scriptures show that many heard the message and believed.

I think of the apostle Stephen, in Acts 7, arrested and put on trial by the Sanhedrin (the religious authorities) in Jerusalem, for his public testimony for Christ. Standing in the court of the synagogue before those who accused him Stephen spoke boldly the word of truth and the Gospel of Christ's salvation. He in essence preached a "fire and brimstone" sermon, recalling the Jews' history as the people of God, challenging them for their disbelief and unfaithfulness, and calling them to faith in Christ. They stoned Him for it in the end, but how many people witnessing that trial heard (and maybe even responded to) the Gospel?

How about Paul, arrested and on trial before King Agrippa, in Acts 26? He was given permission by the king to answer for himself and to respond to the accusations made against him on account of the Gospel of Christ. He gave his personal faith testimony right there in the court of law, essentially calling the king himself to believe in Christ.

> *"'King Agrippa, do you believe the prophets? I know you do.' Then Agrippa said to Paul, 'Do you think that in such a short time you can persuade me to be a Christian'?" (Acts 26:27-28)*

In each instance, and countless more down through the ages, believers turned their persecution into an opportunity to speak boldly for Christ. And we can do the same. In the face of severe opposition and even persecution, God may very well open the door for us to bear witness to our Savior.

And here at long last is my point from the passage above. When that happens, God the Holy Spirit will instruct and enable us to speak.

> *"But when they arrest you, do not worry about what to say or how to say it. At that time you will be given what to say, for it will not be you speaking, but the Spirit of your Father speaking through you." (Matthew 10:20)*

This is God the Son, Jesus, speaking to us about God the Spirit. Remember, Jesus is the second Person of the Holy Trinity. He is God. So when Jesus the Son speaks about the Holy Spirit, it is the same as God the Father saying it. So what does God the Father say here about the God the Holy Spirit?

God says that the Holy Spirit is and will be there with us in those coming times of persecution, telling us what to say when we are given that opportunity. *"But when they arrest you, do not worry about what to say or how to say it."* The King James Version says it: *"take no thought how or what ye shall speak."* It means to have no *"anxious concern, based on apprehension about possible danger or misfortune."*[53]

This is not to say that we can approach our witness to Christ cavalierly or carelessly. We must know the truth ourselves and be very clear about what we believe. We must study the Bible and be well versed in the doctrines of the orthodox Christian faith. We would even do well to have memorized key scriptures so as to be able to call them to mind when needed. As the apostle Peter said it:

> *"But in your hearts set apart Christ as Lord. Always be prepared to give an answer to everyone who asks you to give the reason for the hope that you have." (1 Peter 3:15)*

We need to be prepared, Peter said, to witness for Christ at all times. We need to be ready to speak up and defend our faith in all circumstances.

As a pastor of four different churches over a period of thirty-eight years, I never once entered the pulpit unprepared. I never once thought that

I was free to just stand there and expect the Holy Spirit to, on the spot, give me a sermon to preach. I studied the text for the day to understand its context and meaning when it was written, and how it could/should be applied to our current lives. I relied on God to guide those preparations and later the presentation of the sermon, but I never went into it lightly or unprepared. The same may be said of our testimony, in private or public settings. We need to be as prepared as we possibly can.

At the same time, we do not need to be overly worried about such things, because part of the Holy Spirit's job, so to speak, is to help us and even speak through us sometimes to enable us to have an effective testimony for our Lord. Matthew Henry, in his ageless commentary, said:

> "When you are brought before magistrates, conduct yourselves decently, but afflict not yourselves with care how you shall come off. A prudent thought there must be, but not an anxious, perplexing, disquieting thought … Do not study to make fine speeches … affect not quaint expressions, flourishes of wit, and labored periods."[54]

We have to be thoughtful, prepared, studied and even practiced in our witness, but when the inevitable time comes when we are given opportunity to speak for Him, this passage assures us that the Spirit of God will be there to enable us to speak well and boldly for the truth of the Gospel. We don't need to worry about flowery, dramatic or profound oratory. The Spirit of our heavenly Father will speak through us. That is an encouraging and comforting promise.

The Rev. William Tennat, of New England, once expended much effort to compose an erudite, scholarly sermon. He wanted it to be a great and memorable oratorical masterpiece, because he knew that a famous man, skeptical of the truth of Christianity, would be in attendance that evening.

But when the time came and he attempted to deliver this fine and well-conceived discourse, he became so mixed up and muddled that he couldn't get through it, and was finally compelled to simply stop and close the service by prayer. He was totally embarrassed and disheartened at his very public failure.

However, this unexpected collapse in one who had so often astonished the unbeliever with the force of his eloquence, led the skeptic to think that Mr. Tennat must have been at other times aided by a Divine power. This reflection led to his ultimate conversion. God accomplished by human silence and confusion what his servant wished to do by persuasive preaching. Mr. Tennat afterwards used to say that his confused, disordered and incomplete sermon was one of the most profitable messages that he had ever delivered.[55]

That was an example of the Holy Spirit working through the words of a human to speak to the heart of a skeptic, and convicting him of his need for the Savior. It obviously wasn't the fine and impressive oratory of the preacher that had had such an effect. It was the work of the Spirit of God. It was the Spirit of the Father speaking through him.

I have had experiences such as that. Over the years in pastoral ministry, I have often sought to present fine sermons, with great logic, impeccable Biblical warrant and moving personal illustrations. Such efforts often failed. Could it be that I was trying to make an impression to my own credit, rather than to speak the simple Gospel to glorify Christ? Some of what I regarded as my "best" messages seemed to have very little impact, while others that were in my mind labored and mediocre, I learned later spoke more to people's lives and hearts than I ever imagined. Why was that? Perhaps it was because in the latter instances the Spirit of the Father was at work.

Yes, it's true that we need to guard against those over us: politicians, governors and local councils, who can at times be "cruel and barbarous as beasts, and wholly divested of the thing called humanity."[56] People in authority—spiritually as well as politically—who are supposed to care for and protect us, will use their power to persecute the people of God. It will be a dark and forbidding time indeed.

But God the Holy Spirit will be there with us, strengthening, guiding, helping and instructing. We need to do our homework and be prepared as much as we possibly can. But in the end we don't have to find the perfect, profound words to speak. When we are called before the authorities on account of Christ, and are given the opening to witness for our Lord, the Spirit of the Father Himself will speak through us.

It's not we who will convince and convict anyone in those moments. It will be God Himself. When Robert Morrison, the first missionary to go to China, disembarked from his ship in a Chinese port, the captain sneeringly said, "So you think you are going to make an impression upon China." Morrison quietly replied, "No, sir, but I believe God will."[57]

QUESTIONS FOR CONTEMPLATION OR CONVERSATION

1. Do you think we are in the "end times" leading up to the return of Christ? What makes you think that way?

2. Are you prepared at all times to give an answer for the faith you hold dear? What could you do to be better prepared?

3. Have you ever felt persecuted for your faith? Why? What happened?

4. Do you see the difficulties of living in an unbelieving and antagonistic culture to be a burden or an opportunity? Why?

5. Have you ever been able to turn a difficult situation into an opportunity to witness for Christ? What happened and how did you respond?

CHAPTER 9

The Spirit Gives Birth to Spirit

"Jesus answered, 'I tell you the truth, no one can enter the kingdom of God unless he is born of water and the Spirit. Flesh gives birth to flesh, but the Spirit gives birth to spirit. You should not be surprised at my saying, 'You must be born again.' The wind blows wherever it pleases. You hear its sound, but you cannot tell where it comes from or where it is going. So it is with everyone born of the Spirit'." (John 3:5-8)

Nicodemus was a Pharisee, which to some means he was a hypocrite who demanded that people live by harsh and manifold church rules and regulations which he himself was not willing to obey. We even use the term "pharisaical" to refer to someone who is insufferably self-righteous and who demands strict adherence to formal religious statutes. Certainly that was true of some of the religious leaders of Jesus' day, and He had regular verbal, theological and Biblical battles with them along the way, leading ultimately to His death on the cross at their insistence.

But not *all* Pharisees were like that. We could say something similar about the politicians who rule our nation on the federal and state levels. *Some* are scoundrels who abuse their position for personal gain, to enrich themselves and increase their own power. But not *all*. Many are concerned, selfless public servants who care about their nation and those they represent. It would be a mistake to paint them all with the same broad brush.

So it was with the Biblical era Pharisees. Many were sincere, faithful men who sought the truth and worked hard to serve and please their God.

Nicodemus might be considered one such as that. He had evidently heard about Jesus, His miracles and His teaching, so Nicodemus sought an audience with Jesus to hear for himself from the Master.

He came at night, which is sometimes perceived as a result of fear. Perhaps Nicodemus did not want to be seen consulting such a controversial figure as Jesus who was so hated by many of His peers. Perhaps Nicodemus was afraid of losing his standing among the leaders of the Temple. All that may indeed have been true.

But it could also have simply been that he sought a quiet time away from the crowds, when he could speak to Jesus without interruption. Perhaps he was sincerely seeking the truth.[58] After all, he began the conversation in very respectful terms, calling Jesus "Rabbi," and acknowledging that Jesus had come from God.

> *"Rabbi, we know You are a teacher who has come from God. For no one could perform the miraculous signs You are doing if God were not with Him." (John 3:2)*

In fact, Nicodemus later defended Jesus in the court of the Temple (John 7:50-51) and was criticized by other Pharisees for it. And later still, after Jesus was crucified, Joseph of Arimathea (a secret believer in Jesus from among the Pharisees), with Pilate's permission, came and took the Lord's body down from the cross for burial. He was accompanied by Nicodemus, who brought a mixture of myrrh and aloes. Taking Jesus' body, the two of them wrapped it with the spices, in strips of linen, and carried it to the garden tomb (John 19:38-42). From all the above we could well surmise that Nicodemus was a Pharisee who was, at the very least, a sincere seeker of the truth of God, and not "pharisaical" in any pejorative, derogatory sense.

Without even giving Nicodemus the opportunity to ask a question, Jesus jumped right in:

> *"I tell you the truth, no one can see the kingdom of God unless he is born again." (John 3:3)*

In the King James Version this sentence begins with the words, "Verily, verily." Sometimes the Greek is translated as "Amen." It was a way to put emphasis on what followed. Jesus was saying, "This is important. Hear Me well."

Nicodemus was stunned by what came next. "Huh? What are You talking about? How can a man be born again when he is old? Can he enter into his mother's womb a second time to be born?" (See John 3:4) Nicodemus did not comprehend. Jesus was speaking of spiritual matters, cutting to the very heart of the issue of eternal salvation. Nicodemus took Jesus' words literally and could only think in biological, physical terms. How can one be physically born a second time? Obviously they cannot. But that's not what Jesus was getting at.

I recall an instance many years ago, when I was a freshman in college. I was walking across campus, from my dorm to the chapel, for a midweek evening worship service. Someone stopped me and asked, "Are you a Christian?" I said, "Of course I am. I'm on my way to chapel!" He said, "But are you born again?" Not sure what he meant, I brushed him off and moved along, annoyed at the delay—a reaction very much like Nicodemus'.

What Jesus was saying was that all of us, every human being who ever lived, are dead in our sin. From the very beginning, God warned that sin, any sin, would result in our death.

> *"The LORD God took the man and put him in the Garden of Eden to work it and take care of it. And the LORD God commanded the man, 'You are free to eat from any tree in the garden; but you must not eat from the tree of the knowledge of good and evil, for when you eat of it you will surely die'." (Genesis 2:15-17)*

Adam and Eve disobeyed God from the very first. They did not immediately die physically, but they did die spiritually. And from that moment on, all of humankind inherited a sinful nature and were born spiritually dead as well. That is the continuous testimony of Scripture. Sin leads to death.

> *"For if you live according to the sinful nature, you will die; but if by the Spirit you put to death the misdeeds of the body, you will live." (Romans 8:13)*

"Do not be deceived: God cannot be mocked. A man reaps what he sows. The one who sows to please his sinful nature, from that nature will reap destruction." (Galatians 6:7-8)

"For the wages of sin is death, but the gift of God is eternal life in Christ Jesus our Lord." (Romans 6:23)

"Therefore, just as sin entered the world through one man, and death through sin, and in this way death came to all men, because all sinned." (Romans 5:12)

We are not basically good people, as many like to believe. We are not just slightly smudged or lightly blemished by our sin. We have been defaced, mutilated, disfigured and ruined. *"The wages of sin is <u>death</u>,"* and we are spiritually dead in our sin. We are not slightly off course and in need of some simple directions to get back on track. We are dead. We are not slightly ill, like with the flu or a cold, in need of some sleep and a prescription to be made well. We are dead. We are not generally righteous, moral people who make an occasional mistake and are in need of a mentor to challenge us and call us back into proper line. We are dead, and we need a Savior Redeemer.

When a loved one dies, we hold a funeral service to celebrate their life and say our good-byes, we take them to the local cemetery and we leave them to their final resting place. They cannot, at some later date, decide they want to live again and by their own power come back to life. They are dead, and there is nothing they can do about that by their own capability.

The same is true spiritually. By our sin we die deep down inside, and we cannot by our own power reverse that situation. The effects of sin on human nature are so serious that without the new birth a sinner cannot see, let alone enter into, the kingdom of God.[59]

God is holy and just, totally pure and righteous. Sin cannot exist in His presence. Neither can anyone who is dead in sin. We cannot earn our way into the Kingdom by being reasonably decent people. We can never do enough good deeds to counterbalance the wickedness of our hearts. We are far, far too tainted and marred. Jesus' comment to Nicodemus was a result and a reflection of this truth.

The Spirit Gives Birth to Spirit

The only way, Jesus said, for a person to enter the kingdom of God is to be *reborn* spiritually as pure and righteous people. And this is something we cannot make happen in and of ourselves. I heard the late teacher and theologian R.C. Sproul say many times that a dead person cannot make himself/herself alive again. Contrary to popular horror movies, a dead person is dead. They cannot decide to come back to life and wander the earth like a zombie. They are dead! They are totally helpless and incapable of doing anything for themselves.

As one author aptly put it:

"Christ was sent not to mend wounded people or to wake sleepy people or advise confused people or inspire bored people or spur on lazy people or educate ignorant people, but to raise dead people."[60]

We all need something from beyond ourselves—Someone—to come to our rescue and restore us to life. Jesus answered Nicodemus' incredulous question:

"I tell you the truth, no one can enter the kingdom of God unless he is born of water and the Spirit. Flesh gives birth to flesh, but the Spirit gives birth to spirit. You should not be surprised at my saying, 'You must be born again'." (John 3:5-7)

And here we have God the Son, Jesus, telling us something directly about God the Spirit. This volume is about what God has said about the Holy Spirit. Since Jesus is God, whatever He says about the Spirit comes from God Himself. (See some of our earlier comments on the Trinity.)

And here He tells us something very important about the work of the Holy Spirit in this present age. It is the Spirit of God that gives rebirth to spiritually dead people. It is the Holy Spirit of God that *"gives birth to spirit."* What we cannot do for ourselves, as people with not even a spark of spiritual life in us, the Spirit of God can do. He awakens us and restores our dead spirits to life, so that we can receive and respond to the Gospel of Jesus. Dane Ortlund, in a reflection on John 6:32-40, says:

> *"Divine grace is so radical that it reaches down and turns around our very desires. Our eyes are opened. Christ becomes beautiful. We come to Him. And anyone—'whoever'—is welcome."*[61]

An Old Testament incident recorded in Ezekiel 37 comes to mind. At the time described there, both Israel and Judah (the two halves of the divided Jewish nation) were devastated. The northern kingdom of Israel had been conquered and the people scattered by the Assyrians. Judah, the southern portion of the kingdom, had just been captured by Babylon and those people also carried into exile.

In the midst of these overwhelming national circumstances, the Holy Spirit of God took the prophet Ezekiel and set him in the midst of a valley that was full of dry bones. It was evidently the scene of a horrific battle, and the floor of the valley was literally littered with the dry, dead, unburied, bleached bones of the soldiers who had been killed. It was a vivid image of the total destruction of the Jewish nation!

The Spirit of God said to the prophet, *"Son of man, can these bones live?"* Ezekiel answered, *"O Sovereign Lord, You alone know."* Then the Spirit said to him, *"Prophesy to these bones and say to them, 'Dry bones, hear the word of the Lord! This is what the Sovereign Lord says to these bones: I will make breath enter you, and you will come to life'."* (Ezekiel 37:3–5) And the Spirit caused the bones to come together, flesh to appear and skin to cover them, and He put the breath of life into them so that they came to life. "Through the power of God's Word, the bones came together and formed men, and through the power of the Spirit, life was given to them."[62]

It was an amazing, miraculous vision that foresaw the day in the distant future when the dead nation of Israel would come back to life. The nation was decimated and scattered, and it would take a work of divine might and grace to restore it. That's what God did. This was a prophetic dream that became a reality many centuries later when by the mercy and intervention of God in the affairs of nations, on May 14, 1948, the modern nation of Israel was reborn!

The prophecy in its proper context, of course, was in relation to the nation of Israel. But it also could stand as a vivid metaphor for the spiritual rebirth of a sinner who is dead in their sin, and who is brought back to life by the work of the Holy Spirit of God. If you have responded to the Gospel and put your trust in Jesus as your Savior, it is because, and *only* because, the Holy Spirit worked on your heart to enable you to do so.

Furthermore, as Jesus described it, it is the Holy Spirit who determines where, when and for whom He does this work of new life.

> *"The wind blows wherever it pleases. You hear its sound, but you cannot tell where it comes from or where it is going. So it is with everyone born of the Spirit." (John 3:8)*

It is all done according to the will and the choice of God the Father. God has predestined some for salvation and some for condemnation, some to be saved and others not. Jesus Christ died on the cross to provide atonement for those same elect. The Holy Spirit awakens those whom God has called and for whom Jesus died, and moves them to be converted to the faith of the Christian Gospel, when and how He so chooses.

The big theological term for this is "regeneration." Regeneration is "God's supernatural act of imparting eternal life."[63] As Dr. Wayne Grudem defined it:

> *"Regeneration is a secret act of God in which He imparts new spiritual life to us."*[64]

Since a person is dead in their trespasses and sins and cannot believe, God must first regenerate them in order that they may then be able to have faith. That is the work of the Holy Spirit, as Jesus relates in the text above. Our physical parents gave life to us in the biological realm, according to the will and wisdom of God the Father. The Holy Spirit is the One Who gives us life spiritually. Dr. Grudem went on to say:

> *"Exactly what happens in regeneration is mysterious to us. We know that somehow we who were spiritually dead have been made alive to God and in a very real sense we have been 'born again'."*[65]

All of this raises some important questions. If the only reason we have believed in Jesus as our Savior is the prior, enabling and regenerating work of the Holy Spirit within us, then what cause is there for us to have any pride in our intellectual acumen or our common good sense in taking hold of such a faith? What reason is there to pat ourselves on the back for having deduced this truth and grabbed hold of it? There is none. It is accomplished purely by the grace of God in choosing us as His own and granting new life to our dry, dead bones. It is His initiative and the result of His power at work within us.

The Spirit of God awakened us and breathed spiritual life into us, just as He breathed life into the bones of Ezekiel's valley, and just as He gave life back to the nation of Israel. *"As for you, you were dead in your transgressions and sins,"* Paul said in Ephesians 2:1. But now we are alive, assuming we have trusted in Jesus—*sola gratia, sola fide, sola Christos*. "Only by grace, only through faith, and only in Christ"—as the slogans of the Protestant Reformation stated it.

So our response cannot be spiritual or personal pride in our own goodness, wisdom or common sense. Our only proper response should and must be deep humility and gratitude. Who am I that God would choose me to be one of His, that Jesus would die on the cross to pay the debt of sin that I owe, and that the Holy Spirit would breathe life into my dead spirit enabling me to have faith? To paraphrase Psalm 8:4—"What am I that You are mindful of me, the son of man that You care for me?" Our reasonable response to this grace is to bow before Him in utter amazement at His priceless salvation.

D.L. Moody once quoted Dr. Andrew Bonar (a minister of the *Free Church of Scotland* in the mid to late 1800's), who said that he could tell when a Christian was growing. In proportion to his growth in grace he would elevate his Master, talk less of what he himself was doing, and become smaller and smaller in his own esteem, until, like the morning star, he faded away before the rising sun.[66] That is, or should be, us in response to the amazing grace of God in our salvation.

In John chapter three, early in Jesus' earthly ministry, when John the Baptist was still alive, free and calling people to repentance, John's disciples came to him one day and said, "Teacher, Jesus is also teaching and baptizing and all the people are leaving you and going over to Him." They were upset because John's fame and popularity was being eclipsed by Jesus!

John replied that he had told them he was not the Christ, but merely one sent to witness to the Christ. Jesus was the One, and *"He must become greater; I must become less"* (John 3:26-30). That's what Dr. Bonar was talking about! That should be our attitude of humility and reverence in the face of God's grace to us in Christ.

A second question that may arise, and has for some who have asked it of me over the years, is that if our salvation is solely the initiative of the Spirit of God working within us, then what of those who don't believe? If it all depends on the regenerating work of God the Spirit, then that must mean that He did not (yet) enable a skeptic to believe.

If that is true, then how can a non-believer be held responsible for not believing in Jesus? How can a person be judged guilty of disbelief if the Spirit has not enabled them to understand and receive the Gospel? A person cannot be saved, even if they want to be, unless the Holy Spirit enables them; so, if the Spirit does not enable them, how can they be judged and condemned?

Well, first of all, a person does not even *want* to be saved unless and until the Holy Spirit moves in their heart. Until then, they have no true desire for or thought of God at all. In fact, the Bible describes us before saving faith as outright enemies of God (Romans 5:10, Colossians 1:21).

> *"Once you were alienated from God and were enemies in your minds because of your evil behavior." (Colossians 1:21)*

It is the Holy Spirit in His work of regeneration Who causes and enables us to even desire and then to choose faith in Christ in the first place.

Secondly, to those who claim that this in unfair, we must simply declare, as have many others, that the real question is not why does God save only a select few, but rather why does He save *any* of us at all? We all deserve eternal death and judgment because we are all sinners in rebellion against our heavenly Creator. God is under no compulsion to rescue *any* of us from our situation of dire need. That He does so, for whomever He chooses to do so, is entirely the result of His priceless grace and His divine, sovereign will.

God, in His eternal wisdom and righteous judgment has the perfect right to save whomever He so determines.

A third question has to do with our witness to others. If only those predetermined by God and made alive by the Holy Spirit can respond positively to the Gospel, and we don't know who has been chosen or who has been awakened by the Spirit (and who has not), then how do we know with whom we should share the Good News? Isn't it a waste of time to share the Good News with people who can't possibly receive it because they were not chosen by God to do so?

The answer here is that we have been called and commanded to be witnesses for Jesus Christ, and to tell others the Good News (Matthew 5:13-16, Matthew 28:18-20, Acts 1:8)—period. We are responsible to be faithful to that given task as His ambassadors. *He* is responsible for the results. No, we don't know who is called by God to salvation and who is not, that is clear. But our task is to tell *everyone*, to plant the seeds of the Gospel wherever we go in whomever we meet along the way. And then we allow God to bring forth whatever fruit He desires, in whatever lives His has sovereignly chosen. As someone has wisely said it, "The Christian's responsibility is not to *win* but to witness."[67]

Ours is not to know or to choose who will be saved and who will not. That is up to God alone. Ours is to serve as witnesses to the faith that saved us, and to pray for the Holy Spirit to work in the hearts of those with whom we have shared the Good News. And that is our first and ultimate duty—to pray for the salvation of everyone we love, know and meet. We need to pray for the Holy Spirit to regenerate our family and loved ones, our coworkers, our neighbors and friends, the politicians and leaders who govern us, and many others. We can tell them about Jesus and what He has done for us, but only the Spirit of God can cause them to respond to our witness, so prayer is a must!

This word from Jesus about the work of the Holy Spirit in the salvation of the sinner is cause for great awe and humility to those who have been saved. For those of us who claim Christ as Lord, the only reason we can do so is because God chose us and sent the wind of the Spirit to work in us. Why He did that is beyond understanding. It was a matter of His pure grace, and compels us to give Him our reverence and praise. It also constrains us to testify to His grace everywhere we go, to whomever we meet along the way.

The Duke of Wellington is best known for his defeat of Napoleon at Waterloo. However, one time a young minister asked him for advice as to how he could succeed in the ministry. The Duke asked, "What are your marching orders?" The young man quoted the Great Commission in Matthew 28:19-20. The Duke responded, "Then what are you waiting for?"[68] He could ask that of us today. What are we waiting for?

QUESTIONS FOR CONTEMPLATION OR CONVERSATION

1. Prior to Jesus, did you think of yourself as a basically good person, who may have needed some helpful guidance from God along the way, or did you understand that you were spiritually dead in your sin? How did your perception of yourself inform your relationship with God?

2. How did God show you your need for salvation, and how did He work in your life to draw you to Christ?

3. How would you respond if someone asked if you were "born again"? Assuming you are born again, how does it make you feel that God chose you before the beginning of time to be one of His own, and sent the Holy Spirit to regenerate you so that you could turn to Him?

4. Is it easy or difficult for you to talk to others about Kingdom related matters, or to share your faith with them? Why?

5. What has been your experience in sharing Jesus with others? How does that affect your willingness to do so again?

CHAPTER 10

Another Counselor

"If you love Me, you will obey what I command. And I will ask the Father, and He will give you another Counselor to be with you forever—the Spirit of truth. The world cannot accept Him, because it neither sees Him nor knows Him. But you know Him, for He lives with you and will be in you." (John 14:15-17)

We have been studying what God has said about the Holy Spirit, and have looked at many passages in the Bible where God the Father (the "first" Person of the divine Trinity) spoke directly about God the Spirit (the "third" Person of the divine Trinity). In the previous chapter we acknowledged that Jesus (the "second" Person of the divine Trinity) is also God, so that whatever the Son says about the Spirit is the same as if God the Father said it. And in that section we saw that Jesus explained our need for the regenerating work of the Spirit in our hearts to make us alive to the things of God.

What else did God the Son say about God the Spirit? For that we remain in the Gospel of John, but jump ahead to chapter 14. Jesus and His disciples were in Jerusalem, celebrating the Passover Feast—His last on earth with them. The crucifixion was just hours ahead, the evening meal had been served and Judas had already decided to betray Jesus, though he had not yet gone to do so. Jesus took a towel and basin to humbly wash the disciples' feet as He began to prepare them for what was to come.

Jesus predicted His betrayal, their denial and desertion of Him, and sent Judas away to do his dastardly deed. Then, in John 14-17, Jesus began to share some last teachings with His friends and to pray for Himself, the disciples and all believers to come. If you have a "red letter" Bible, which denotes the words of Jesus with red print, these four chapters of John's Gospel are pretty much all in red, with just a few exceptions.

He began, amazingly enough, by attempting to comfort them, knowing what they would be facing in the coming hours and days. Can you imagine that! Jesus was facing a horrific ordeal Himself. He was about to be betrayed, arrested, denied, deserted, falsely accused, beaten, mocked, scourged and finally crucified. We cannot even imagine the physical pain and emotional heartache He would bear—and that all alone. He knew full well what was coming, and yet there Jesus was comforting the very people who would run away and leave Him to His tormentors. Isn't that just like our Lord? The deepest concern of His heart in that moment was not Himself, but His disciples.

It makes me think—could that be the way Jesus treats *me*? When I betray Him, deny Him, disobey His Word, is it possible that He treats me with the same care and compassion He showed to His disciples on the eve of His crucifixion? Is His love so deep, His grace so high, that He would even show compassion to one such as I? Like the old Charles Wesley hymn says it:

> *And can it be that I should gain*
> *An interest in the Savior's blood?*
> *Died He for me, who caused His pain*
> *For me, who Him to death pursued? Amazing love!*
> *How can it be that Thou, my God, shouldst die for me?*

I bow in humble gratitude before Him, knowing that His grace covers even my sin and shame. The same is true for you, and for all who have trusted in Him as their Savior. As Paul prayed, so I pray for you, my dear reader:

> *"And I pray that you, being rooted and established in love, may have power, together with all the saints, to grasp how wide and long and high and deep is the love of Christ, and to know this love that surpasses knowledge—that you may be filled to the measure of all the fullness of God." (Ephesians 3:17-19)*

As Jesus sought to encourage and strengthen them for the coming ordeal, He described for them the home that awaited them in the glory of God's eternal Kingdom that He Himself was going to prepare for them. He assured them that they would do great works for God and that He would be standing by, a prayer away, to help them accomplish unbelievable miracles.

And then, in the text quoted above, God the Son spoke again about the promise of God the Holy Spirit. He said:

> *"If you love Me, you will obey what I command. And I will ask the Father, and He will give you another Counselor to be with you forever—the Spirit of Truth." (John 14:15-17a)*

Here we see several critical truths about the Holy Spirit. We will look briefly at them, not necessarily in order.

First of all, we need to understand the name Jesus used for the Spirit—"Counselor." What does that mean? The Greek word is *Paraclete,* which is used only by the apostle John (John 14:16, 26; 15:26; 16:7).[69] It is a word that is a bit difficult to define because it has such a wide range of possible meanings and uses.[70] Hence, it is translated into the English in a variety of ways: "Counselor" in the New International Version, "Helper" in the New American Standard Version and "Comforter" in the King James Version. Perhaps we could say that all contain a portion of the full meaning.

"Counselor" could be perceived as a legal term, and is often used as such in our court system. At least in the TV shows featuring court settings, the lawyers, especially for the defense, are often called "Counselor." These attorneys counsel or advise their clients concerning legal procedures and the best way to mount their defense.

But this term could apply to a variety of settings in which someone is there for us to offer guidance, correction and direction, such as a therapist advising a troubled person how to deal with their internal or relational issues, or a guidance counselor in a school helping a student chart the course of their life and career in years to come. That is certainly part of the work of the Holy Spirit.

While Jesus was on earth with His disciples, *He* was their ultimate "Counselor." He certainly was the One who guided and directed them, showed them the right way, advised them on proper attitudes and behaviors and even corrected them when the occasion called for it—which it did numerous times. So Jesus was promising that even in His absence they would have another to provide this range of assistance as they moved forward into their ministries.

"Comforter" describes a very specific role of encouraging and sympathizing in times of sorrow or affliction. The English word comes from two Latin words meaning "with strength." This implies more than simply consolation or sympathy, it speaks of someone who strengthens us to face life's hardships with courage and keep on keeping on.[71]

Isaiah 40 is an expression of it. Through His prophet, God had just spoken a frightening word of judgment and wrath. The time was coming when the palace in Jerusalem will be overrun and destroyed, all of its wealth and its beautiful decorations will be taken away, and the people of the nation carried off to exile in Babylon. *"'Nothing will be left,' says the* L*ord*. *'And some of your descendants, your own flesh and blood who will be born to you, will be taken away, and they will become eunuchs in the palace of the king of Babylon'."* (Isaiah 39:5-8) It was a word of devastating and sorrowful impact.

But God immediately followed that harsh and painful message with one of great comfort and hopefulness.

> *"Comfort, comfort My people,*
> *says your God.*
> *Speak tenderly to Jerusalem,*
> *and proclaim to her*
> *that her hard service has been completed,*
> *that her sin has been paid for,*
> *that she has received from the* L*ord*'s *hand*
> *double for all her sins."* (Isaiah 40:1-2)

What consolation that must have given to those who heard it! Difficult, tragic days are coming, but God is not finished! How their hearts must have soared to know that He would one day vindicate and rescue His people. It was a word of such hope that people down through the ages have turned to it in time of need.

Handel began his classic work, "Messiah," with those very words: "Comfort ye." Luther pored over it when in exile in the castle at Salzburg. John Brown read it in prison at Harper's Ferry. Oliver Cromwell went to it for help in time of storm. Daniel Webster read it again and again when he was crushed and broken in spirit. Tennyson called it one of the five great classics in the Old Testament record.[72] Part of the work of the Holy Spirit is to be our Comforter.

The term "Helper" seems to me to be a broader term that might encompass all of the above. The Holy Spirit helps us with guidance, comfort, correction, consolation and much more. As Jamieson, Fausset and Brown explain:

> "A term such as 'Helper' is highly generic and can be particularly useful in some languages. In certain instances, for example, the concept of 'Helper' is expressed idiomatically, for example, 'the one who mothers us' or, as in one language in Central Africa, 'the one who falls down beside us,' that is to say, an individual who upon finding a person collapsed along the road, kneels down beside the victim, cares for his needs, and carries him to safety."[73]

The image that comes immediately to mind here is Jesus' parable in Luke 10:30-36. A man was set upon by bandits and left by the side of the road to die. Others walked by unmoved and unwilling to "get involved." But a Samaritan came along, saw the man and at once sprang into action. He went to him and bandaged his wounds, pouring on oil and wine. Then he put the man on his own donkey, took him to an inn and personally took care of him. When he had to continue his journey, he paid the innkeeper to look after this poor fellow. There was a man who knelt beside the wounded traveler and cared for the full range of his needs.

That is an image of the "Helper" promised by Jesus to the disciples, and to us. The Holy Spirit of God will come to render aid to us in a wide variety of ways, and will help us along the pathway of our lives. We are never alone. We have such a "Helper" to assist, guide and comfort. How encouraging it is to know that God the Spirit is always with us and always lifting, guiding, strengthening, and even carrying us in His mighty arms.

Jesus said two more important things here that we must notice. In verse 17 Jesus specifically called Him "the Spirit of Truth." God is the God of truth:

> *"Into Your hands I commit my spirit; redeem me, O LORD, the God of truth." (Psalm 31:5)*

> *"For the word of the LORD is right and true; He is faithful in all He does." (Psalm 33:4)*

Jesus, as the Son of God and the second Person of the Trinity, claimed the same for Himself: *"I am the way and the truth and the life. No one comes to the Father except through Me."* (John 14:6)

So it only stands to reason that the Holy Spirit, along with the Father and the Son, is truth. As Matthew Henry said it:

> He is the *Spirit of truth.* He will be true to you ...He will *teach you the truth,* will enlighten your minds with the knowledge of it, will strengthen and confirm your belief of it, and will increase your love to it. The Gentiles by their idolatries, and the Jews by their traditions, were led into gross errors and mistakes; but the Spirit of truth shall not only *lead you into all truth,* but others by your ministry. Christ is the truth, and He is the Spirit of Christ.[74]

Just as God is truth and Jesus is truth, so the Holy Spirit is truth. It is who He is. It is His character and being. He never lies—He cannot lie. He always leads us in the way of God's truth and will remind us of that divine truth as we seek it and whenever or for whatever reason we need it.

Over the years of our ministry, we heard several people say, as they embarked upon a course that was clearly unbiblical and sinful, that they had a peace in their heart about this that they believed came from the Holy Spirit. Well, they may have had a sense of sereneness in their hearts, but it was definitely NOT from the Holy Spirit of God. God does not contradict

Himself or His Word. If the Bible clearly speaks against something you are tempted to do (either directly or in principle), no matter how peaceful you may inwardly feel about it, the Holy Spirit will never confirm that in your heart. That is not who He is.

At that point, you may need to reevaluate your decision. If it is contrary to the spoken, written Word of God, then it did not come from the counsel of the Holy Spirit. Perhaps it reflects the desires of your own heart. Maybe it comes from the enemy of your soul, trying to lead you astray. It could be the pull of the values and thinking of the world around you, tempting you to compromise your Christian ideals. In any case, God the Spirit will never propose or confirm anything contrary to the clear will of God the Father.

And finally let's note one last thing Jesus said here:

"The world cannot accept Him, because it neither sees Him nor knows Him. But you know Him, for He lives with you and will be in you." (John 14:17)

"He lives with you and will be in you." What an amazing thought! During Jesus' earthly life He walked with and talked to His disciples. He was Immanuel, *"which means God with us."* (Matthew 1:23) Literally, physically, and visibly, Jesus was with them. They saw Him, touched Him, ate meals with Him, learned from Him, most likely laughed with Him at some of the funny stories He told. How amazing must that have been?

Nowadays, people make pilgrimages to Israel, and afterwards talk about how life-changing it was for them to see places where Jesus was, and to visit likely scenes of Biblical events. We've never been able to do that, but it sounds wonderful to visit such sacred places—made sacred because of the presence of Jesus, two millennia ago.

But after Jesus' ascension, God the Holy Spirit, the Spirit of Jesus, actually came to live not just alongside but literally *within* the hearts of those who believe. He will be with us and even *within* us who have believed. When the Spirit regenerates us and enables us to respond in faith, at the moment of our decision for Christ He comes to live in our hearts. It can't get any closer than that. Pentecostal theology speaks of a "baptism of the Spirit" that occurs separately from conversion. One has to seek and ask for God to grant this coming of the Holy Spirit into their life.

Orthodox evangelical doctrine holds that the baptism of the Spirit occurs at the moment of conversion. "The baptism of the Spirit occurs at conversion when the Spirit enters the believing sinner, gives him new life, and makes his body the temple of God. *All* believers have experienced this once-for-all baptism (1 Corinthians 12:13). Nowhere does the Scripture command us to *seek* this baptism, because we have already experienced it and it need not be repeated."[75] If you are a true believer in the Gospel of Christ, you have the Spirit of God in your heart, closer than the closest friend.

Now, it must quickly be added that this baptism of the Spirit at the moment of faith does not necessarily mean that we are "filled" by the Spirit, or that we from then on live with a total and complete faithfulness and obedience to Him. We spend the rest of our earthly lives learning to live under the Spirit's control and growing in the fullness of that Spirit; or at least we should. But that connection will never be total until we are glorified and God completes His work in us.

> *"... being confident of this, that He who began a good work in you will carry it on to completion until the day of Christ Jesus." (Philippians 1:6)*

I have been a Christian now for nearly fifty years. I sincerely hope, that I have grown and matured from that early, hesitating, uninformed faith commitment into a more knowledgeable, faithful and established follower of the Lord. I hope—I think—I have come a long way in those five decades as I gradually learned more and more what it is to know and love God. *"Not that I have already obtained all this, or have already been made perfect, but I press on to take hold of that for which Christ Jesus took hold of me."* (Philippians 3:12) I pray the same for you, as you move along in your own journey with Him.

Until that day comes when He completes the work His has been doing in us, may we all continue to grow in the grace and knowledge of the Lord and Savior Jesus Christ (2 Peter 3:18), and allow the Holy Spirit to fill us in ever expanding degrees. In this way we will know the counsel, comfort and help He offers more and more, and be able to live more fully in submission to Him.

QUESTIONS FOR CONTEMPLATION OR CONVERSATION

1. How have you experienced the counsel of the Holy Spirit in your own walk of faith? His comfort? His help?

2. Have you ever misinterpreted guidance you have received to be from the Spirit of God, when it in fact was not His? How did that occur, and what was the result?

3. Have you ever visited Israel and seen the places where Jesus lived and walked? How did that make you feel? If not, would you like to do so? Why?

4. What does it say to you that He is the "Spirit of Truth"? How can you live that reality in your daily life?

5. Do you realize that the Holy Spirit lives within you and has been there since the day you believed? How completely do you believe you are filled by that Spirit? Why?

6. What could you do to live more fully under the Spirit's control and power?

CHAPTER 11

Teacher and Reminder

"Jesus replied, 'If anyone loves Me, he will obey My teaching. My Father will love him, and We will come to him and make Our home with him. He who does not love Me will not obey My teaching. These words you hear are not My own; they belong to the Father who sent Me.

"All this I have spoken while still with you. But the Counselor, the Holy Spirit, whom the Father will send in My name, will teach you all things and will remind you of everything I have said to you. Peace I leave with you; My peace I give you. I do not give to you as the world gives. Do not let your hearts be troubled and do not be afraid'." (John 14:23-27)

To fully understand the sentences above from the Word of God, we must begin by taking note that what Jesus said is a description of what takes place within a proper relationship between the follower of Christ and the divine God above. He is the sovereign Creator, Lord and Savior, Ruler of all things and Master of our lives. We are to live in total submission to His dictates and will, as ones who have been chosen by God, redeemed by Christ and regenerated by the Holy Spirit. By the initiating work of God, we have been saved from death and given new life in the Spirit.

Ours is to humbly submit to Him and obey His Word. Notice that Jesus said if anyone loves Him (Jesus), they will obey His Word—and *then* God the Father and Son would take up residence within them. Why would the holy God take up residence within people who by their disregard and disobedience put themselves in relationship with Him as God's enemy or antagonist? That would not make sense.

Jesus spoke plainly to this very issue in Matthew 7. He said, in essence, that true faith is not just in claiming Christ as our Savior and Lord, we also have to live in daily obedience to His Word and commands. He said:

> *"Not everyone who says to Me, 'Lord, Lord,' will enter the kingdom of heaven, but only he who does the will of My Father who is in heaven. Many will say to Me on that day, 'Lord, Lord, did we not prophesy in Your name, and in Your name drive out demons and perform many miracles?' Then I will tell them plainly, 'I never knew you. Away from Me, you evildoers'!" (Matthew 7:21-23)*

He also said:

> *"Why do you call Me, 'Lord, Lord,' and do not do what I say?"*
> *(Luke 6:46)*

Those who daily reject His love and rule in their lives have no promise of the presence of the Holy Spirit. It is within those who love and therefore *obey* Him that Jesus promises to make His abode. As we yield more and more of our hearts and lives to God, and progressively learn to know and follow His Word, our relationship with Him grows deeper and closer. His presence within becomes more real to us. Our lives come to be more in tune with His will. Our obedience becomes more natural and necessary to us. And it is within that kind of growing relationship of submission that Jesus speaks further to His disciples about the promise of the Holy Spirit.

At this point in time, Jesus was still personally present with the apostles. But in just a few hours He would be suddenly and brutally separated from them by those who hated Him, and the time was coming when His friends would see Him no more. Nevertheless, Jesus promised that God the Father would send another *"Counselor"* (John 14:26) to be with them and to guide them. There's that name we discussed in the last chapter: the Greek word *Paraclete,* which we saw translated as "Counselor," "Helper" and "Comforter."

Given the circumstances in which this comment was made, I think "Counselor" is the translation that makes most sense here in the text at the head of this chapter. Jesus promised that this Counselor, the Holy Spirit, would teach them all things and would remind them of everything He had said to them. We must not glance over these words too lightly, they are important.

As I was reminded recently in a Ligonier Ministry podcast with Dr. Sinclair Ferguson, Jesus specifically spoke these promises to His disciples, and we dare not try to understand them apart from that context. The disciples were frail and weak. There was much they did not yet understand, in spite of Jesus' herculean effort to instruct and enlighten them over the past three years. There were many times when what Jesus tried to explain to them went completely over their heads. He was often speaking to them of spiritual realities and they bogged down in a worldly mindset.

The examples are many—here's just one. In Matthew 15-16, Jesus fed four thousand men, along with many women and children, using seven loaves of bread and a few small fish. When all had eaten and were satisfied, the disciples picked up seven baskets full of broken pieces that were left over. After Jesus had sent the crowd away, He got into the boat and went on to the next town.

As they were crossing the lake, the disciples realized they had forgotten to take bread. *"Be careful,"* Jesus said to them. *"Be on your guard against the yeast of the Pharisees and Sadducees"* (Matthew 16:6). The disciples discussed this amongst themselves, trying to figure out what Jesus was talking about. It seemed to make no sense at all. Hearing their confusion, Jesus asked,

> *"You of little faith, why are you talking among yourselves about having no bread? Do you still not understand?" (Matthew 16:8-9)*

Do you *still* not understand? How many times in the Gospels did the apostles misinterpret or totally misunderstand what Jesus was trying to tell them? There were too many, showing them to be quite dense at times. For other examples of this, see—Matthew 19:25; Mark 4:13, 6:51-52, 8:17-18, 9:32; Luke 9:45; John 4:32-33, 10:6, 11:12-13, 16:18, 20:9. While Jesus was with them, there was much the apostles did not fully grasp or remember.

In all fairness, let's not think we would have done any better had we been in their shoes. Jesus was speaking to them of profound, heavenly truths that went way beyond anything they had ever heard before. It would have been just as mindboggling to us as it was to them. We would most likely have been just as dense and confused as they were.

Furthermore, they did not yet have the Holy Spirit residing in their hearts, as we now do, so they did not have that inner assistance opening their eyes and minds to God's Word. That makes all the difference!

Nevertheless, Jesus said, in the text above, that when He left them He would send another Counselor, Who would teach them all things and remind them of everything He had taught them. This was crucial for the birth of the Church in years to come. After the crucifixion and resurrection of Jesus, things began to make more sense to the apostles, things that had eluded them earlier. It was that Counselor, the Holy Spirit, Who began to clarify and illuminate things Jesus had said and done, and to help them put those things in proper perspective.

In the midst of the great excitement and celebration of Jesus' arrival into Jerusalem, on what we now call "Palm Sunday," John inserted an almost parenthetical statement:

> *"At first His disciples did not understand all this. Only after Jesus was glorified did they realize that these things had been written about Him and that they had done these things to Him." (John 12:16)*

Only after Jesus died and was raised were the apostles able to properly add things up and come to grips with what they had seen and heard. And that was only with the help of the Counselor—the Holy Spirit of God. He was the one who taught them all things and helped them to understand what before had been totally unintelligible to them.

It was through the Holy Spirit's enabling that they were able to teach the truth of the Gospel to the infant church they helped to plant. It was the Spirit within them that helped them to rightly interpret, explain and teach that truth with effective, timeless clarity. As Matthew Henry said it in his commentary:

As a Spirit of wisdom and revelation Christ was a teacher to His disciples; if He leave them now that they have made so little proficiency, what will become of them? Why, the Spirit shall teach them, shall be their standing Tutor. He shall teach them all things necessary for them either to learn themselves, or to teach others. For those that would teach the things of God must first themselves be taught of God; this is the Spirit's work.[76]

It was that same Counselor, the Holy Spirit, who enabled them to remember the stories and words of Christ accurately when it came to putting that Gospel in written form. Jesus specifically said that this new Counselor will remind them of everything He had said to them. This was certainly not only for their comfort and assurance. It was to inform their teaching and preaching, and it was an absolute necessity for them to receive the inspiration to write the Holy Scripture. Those who wrote the Gospels were not just working from fallible, limited human memory.

If there is an accident or a crime with several witnesses, the investigators are sure to hear multiple and varied versions of the same scene. All the witnesses were there at the time in question, all saw the same incident, but they will most likely all remember different details and even different perceptions of what happened, based on their own individual interpretation of what happened. The late Dr. David Powlison used to often say that we live our lives based not on reality, but on our interpretation of reality. Such is the case with witnesses to an accident.

In the instance of the writing of the Gospels, the authors were relying not only on their own weak and uncertain human memories and personal interpretations of their perceptions, they had the powerful assistance of the Holy Spirit of God to remind them of everything Jesus said and did. Those who argue against the integrity and reliability of the Bible usually ignore or discount the element of the Spirit's counsel in the process. The Bible can be trusted because it was written under the guidance and inspiration of the Spirit of God.

"All Scripture is God-breathed and is useful for teaching, rebuking, correcting and training in righteousness." (2 Timothy 3:16)

So Jesus' promise to His apostles was critical for the teaching and writing they would be called upon to perform.

The first thing we have to understand with this text is the context in which it was spoken. Jesus said these words directly to and for the express benefit of His apostles, who would need the help of the Counselor in very specific and personal ways. But how then can we understand what it might say *to us*? Do we just discount it as not applying to us in this day and age, or can we find meaning from it for our own situations?

I believe that there can be many layers to the Scriptures, and this is certainly one such example. Many of the Old Testament prophecies, for example, spoke directly to the generation in which they were given, warning the people of dire events and judgments they would face in their lifetimes, or offering encouragements to the hearers of God's help and hope *at that time*. And yet many of the prophecies also spoke of events that would unfold centuries into the future. Many were fulfilled in the era in which they were given but also, in another sense, in ages to come. Many prophecies and psalms spoke of the human king, David, but also on another level of the eternal King, Jesus.

In this text, while we remember that the initial message was one of hope and help for the apostles of Jesus for their life and ministry to come, we can also see that there are messages for us in our day and age. Such is the depth, wisdom and applicability of Scripture.

So what might be the lessons for us—in addition to the reliability and infallibility of the Scriptures themselves, mentioned above? First of all, on a fundamental level, the Spirit of God convinces and convicts us of the reliability and inerrancy of the Scriptures themselves. It is the Spirit of God that validates and confirms the truth of God's Word and compels us to believe it. As one biographer of John Bunyan put it:

> Bunyan received the Bible not as the words of men but as the Word of God … Therefore, God's own majesty thunders in His Word … The majesty of Scripture shines in its truthfulness and inerrancy … The Bible is the only solid basis for our beliefs.[77]

From where does such a firm conviction come? It comes only from the work of the Spirit of God within a believer. A non-believer, without the Spirit of God in their heart, will find it hard—if not impossible—to understand the divine nature and reliability of the Bible. There is a growing disregard and even disdain for the Bible in our post-Christian culture. The secular, unbelieving world sees it as archaic, contradictory and confusing. But the Counselor Jesus promised to those who trust and obey Him is a present help to those who believe, affirming and confirming that trust in His Holy Word over and over.

Secondly, I believe this description of the Counselor tells us that the Holy Spirit is within us to help us to rightly perceive, interpret and apply God's Word. As we read the Bible, the Spirit of God is there to instruct us, open our minds and hearts, and help us to discern God's Word *to us*.

Certainly we must make a careful study of the Scriptures, using all the resources available to us, to make certain we are seeing things in their proper context and understanding them based on an accurate view of the words we are reading. We cannot just assume that we, by our own personal wisdom and knowledge, can always determine the true meaning and reasoning of the passages we read. Solid, faithful resources abound, from good, evangelical Biblical scholars to help us understand the historical and cultural background, language nuances and cross references to help us make good sense of a particular passage.

And we should avail ourselves of such input to make sure we do not get too far off track from a reasonable understanding of the Scriptures. History is littered with cult leaders who have taken Bible passages out of context and twisted them to suit their own desires or viewpoints, leading many thousands astray. Their teachings can often sound quite reasonable because they are quoting the Bible. But they subtly make them to say something quite different from what a sound analysis would explain. They still do that to this day, perhaps more than ever. So a careful, reasoned, informed study of the Bible is essential.

At the same time, it is also true that a person can prayerfully approach the Scriptures with faithful openness to the Spirit of God, and can receive from God His clear word to them for that day and time. How often have you been reading your Bible and been deeply struck by something in it that you felt was coming directly to you and to your current situation? It may have been a passage that you had read many times before with little notice or impact. But this time it profoundly spoke to you with a correction, encouragement or direction you sorely needed. That is the work of the Counselor, the teacher Jesus promised, helping us to rightly interpret the Word of God for our lives.

The great pastor and teacher Charles Haddon Spurgeon told often of being converted to the faith by a preacher he had heard who, having nothing else to say that day, simply repeated his text over and over. The smoldering Words of God burned deeply into Spurgeon's heart and compelled him to a life of faithful and effective service to the Kingdom of God.[78] I suggest that we need a balanced approach to our study and use of God's Word. We need to do a careful analysis using relevant and trustworthy study resources, while at the same time trusting and relying on the Holy Spirit to illuminate and apply it to our personal life and situation.

And thirdly, I believe it is the work of the Holy Spirit to remind us of God's Word in situations where it is most needed. Perhaps when we have a difficult decision to make, the Spirit will recall to our mind a passage from the Bible that speaks directly to the situation in question. It may be, as we talk with others about our faith, and they raise a question that has troubled them, God the Spirit will direct our thoughts to the passages necessary to help them find the answers.

Maybe the day will come when you are called to answer for your faith—perhaps in a group of skeptical family members, friends or coworkers, conceivably even in a court of law. Many have faced such a trial before powers and authorities. As we discussed in chapter 8, Jesus said:

> *"But when they arrest you, do not worry about what to say or how to say it. At that time you will be given what to say, for it will not be you speaking, but the Spirit of your Father speaking through you." (Matthew 10:19-20)*

Often the early disciples were hauled before the religious and/or civil authorities for preaching Christ, and they always seemed to give powerful testimonies to the truth of the Gospel, often quoting the Scriptures to do so. How could they do that under such stressful circumstances? It was the

Holy Spirit, the Counselor and Teacher promised by Jesus, Who provided the words and the testimony. He will do the same for us, as we rely on and trust in Him.

But that points us right back to our need to be reading, studying and even memorizing Scripture. For the Holy Spirit to *remind* us of relevant passages, we must first have read, studied and learned those passages. There must be a library of Biblical truths and passages in our minds and hearts for Him to bring them to our recollection. That depends upon us.

As one author put it:

> [Many] Americans and other Westerners claim to have read all or part of the Bible. However, when asked to identify even four books of the Bible or four of Jesus' disciples or four of the Ten Commandments, fewer than half even attempt to respond and fewer than one in ten respond correctly.[79]

That forms a sad commentary on the general Biblical illiteracy of the church today. On the other hand, there were these faithful believers:

> Tertullian devoted his days and nights to Bible reading, so much so that he learned much of it by heart, even its punctuations.
>
> Theodosius the Younger could repeat any part of the Scripture exactly, and discourse with the bishops at court as if he himself were a bishop.
>
> Eusebius said that he heard of one, whose eyes were burned out under the Diocletian persecution, repeat from memory the Scriptures in a large assembly.
>
> Beza could repeat all Paul's epistles in Greek at age 80.
>
> Cramer could repeat the entire New Testament from memory, learning it on his journey to Rome.
>
> Ridley also memorized the entire New Testament during his walks in the Pembroke Hall of Cambridge.[80]

Our challenge is to read, contemplate and store God's Word in our hearts so that we can remember it—or so the Counselor can remind us of it—whenever it would inform and benefit those to whom we happen to be speaking.

We can boldly speak the Word of God into the situations of our lives. We can calmly witness to family and friends of our salvation in Christ. We can courageously stand for Kingdom truths and values in the "marketplace of ideas," even when that may be rather unpopular. As we learn more and more of God's Word, and trust increasingly in our Counselor, the Holy Spirit of God, assisting, teaching and reminding us from within, we need not fear or shrink from opportunities to firmly and warmly speak for Christ. We can, as a friend used to say, *"Live large with God in charge."*

QUESTIONS FOR CONTEMPLATION OR CONVERSATION

1. Do you have what scholars would call a "high view of Scripture" (trusting fully in its Divine source, inspiration and inerrancy) or what they would call a "low view of Scripture" (seeing it as the result of faulty, personal memories of Jesus and human deductions about God)? Why?

2. How have you experienced the presence of the Holy Spirit in your life? What changes or results did that produce in your life and faith?

3. Can you recall situations in which you were sure that the Counselor had helped you to remember Scriptural principles or truths, or even actual Bible passages, to help you answer critics or comfort fellow believers? What were some of those circumstances?

4. How have you stored up Scriptures in your heart so that they are there for the Spirit of God to bring to your memory as needed?

5. Do you feel that you can speak boldly for your faith, or are you hesitant? Why? What would it take to help you be more assured?

CHAPTER 12

The One Who Convicts and Convinces

"But I tell you the truth: It is for your good that I am going away. Unless I go away, the Counselor will not come to you; but if I go, I will send Him to you. When He comes, He will convict the world of guilt in regard to sin and righteousness and judgment: in regard to sin, because men do not believe in Me; in regard to righteousness, because I am going to the Father, where you can see Me no longer; and in regard to judgment, because the prince of this world now stands condemned." (John 16:7-11)

God the Father, through Jesus the Son, had more to say about God the Holy Spirit. We turn now to the Gospel of John, chapter 16. This is still part of Jesus' last discourse to His disciples, in the "Upper Room," just before going to the Mount of Olives where He was arrested. Jesus was still trying to comfort, encourage and instruct His friends to prepare them for the difficult ordeal to come, and for His ultimate departure from this earth. In order to do so, Jesus returned again and again to the promise of the Holy Spirit.

Here Jesus said that it would ultimately be to their benefit that He would go away. Can you imagine that? The One they loved above all others; the One in Whom they had found life and meaning; the One Who had guided them on the pathway of faith and righteousness—was soon to leave them. On some level, in spite of their general obtuseness, I would guess that they sensed the gravity and seriousness of Jesus' words and mood at that Last Supper. Surely they knew something profoundly dramatic and shattering was about to happen. And then, on top of that, Jesus told them He would leave them.

BUT, Jesus said, it would be a good thing for them that He did! "Seriously?" they must have thought. "Are you kidding? How can we possibly manage without You?" Previously, when Jesus began to tell people about His coming death, many turned away and no longer followed Him. Jesus asked the twelve if they wanted to leave Him as well. Peter responded:

> *"Lord, to whom shall we go? You have the words of eternal life. We believe and know that You are the Holy One of God." (John 6:68-69)*

I would guess that similar thoughts raced through their minds now. Where will we go? What will we do if Jesus leaves us? He is the One we believe in and trust. Jesus is the one and only Holy One of God. He is the One who has the words of God and of eternity. What will we do now?

The answer, Jesus assured them, is coming. I will send to you the Counselor, the Holy Spirit, and He will care for you, empower you, instruct you and guide you in ways you cannot even conceive. He used one particular word in this instance to describe what the Spirit of God will do—<u>convict</u>. *"When He comes, He will convict the world ..."* (John 16:8).

The Greek word is *elencho* (ἐλέγχω). It means "to state that someone has done wrong, with the implication that there is adequate proof of such wrongdoing—to rebuke, to reproach."[81] Luke used the same word to describe how John the Baptist rebuked Herod the tetrarch for his marriage to Herodias, his brother's wife (Luke 3:19). Paul used it to instruct the Ephesians to have nothing to do with those who engage in sinful, fruitless deeds of darkness, saying they should instead expose them (Ephesians 5:11).

One key function of the Holy Spirit of God is to convict and rebuke.

> *"When He comes, He will convict the world of guilt in regard to sin and righteousness and judgment: in regard to sin, because men do not believe in Me; in regard to righteousness, because I am going to the Father, where you can see Me no longer; and in regard to judgment, because the prince of this world now stands condemned." (John 16:8-11)*

In short, one primary work of the Holy Spirit of God is to bring conviction of sin to unbelievers and convince them of their need for the Savior, Jesus. The ultimate purpose is not to condemn—but to save.

First, the Holy Spirit works in people's hearts to make them aware of their sin. This is a necessary first step. Few people understand how sinful they really are. Go into any jail or prison in the land and you will be hard pressed to find more than a handful of those incarcerated who will acknowledge that they deserve to be there. Most will loudly profess their innocence, even after they were convicted in a court of law with overwhelming evidence proving their guilt.

That attitude is equally true of the average non-incarcerated citizen who is simply working, living and doing the best they can. Most believe that, certainly, they make mistakes here and there. But basically they are certain that they are good people and God will accept them as such. Most people these days believe that you get into heaven by being a good person, and that they are unquestionably good enough to make the cut. They are not. No one is.

"There is not a righteous man on earth who does what is right and never sins." So says the Bible at Ecclesiastes 7:20. Wow, that's pretty harsh, isn't it? Not a single truly righteous man—or woman or child—on earth who never sins. Really? What about Mother Theresa? What about Billy Graham? What about ... fill in the blank with the name of anyone you consider to be an unusually pious and righteous person, past or present. Even the very best of us never perfectly do what is right and never sin.

That is the consistent testimony of scripture. Consider the following, for just a sample:

> *"The LORD looks down from heaven on the sons of men to see if there are any who understand, any who seek God. All have turned aside, they have together become corrupt; there is no one who does good, not even one."* (Psalm 14:2-3)

> *"Surely I was sinful at birth, sinful from the time my mother conceived me."* (Psalm 51:5)

> *"If you, O LORD, kept a record of sins, O Lord, who could stand?"* (Psalm 130:3)

> *"Who can say, 'I have kept my heart pure; I am clean and without sin'?" (Proverbs 20:9)*

> *"There is no one righteous, not even one; there is no one who understands, no one who seeks God. All have turned away, they have together become worthless; there is no one who does good, not even one." (Romans 3:10-12)*

The Scriptures are clear—there is no human being ever, anywhere, who has not been conceived in sin and who has not continuously lived in sin. Save one, and only one—Jesus.

> *"God made Him who had no sin to be sin for us, so that in Him we might become the righteousness of God." (2 Corinthians 5:21)*

> *"For we do not have a high priest who is unable to sympathize with our weaknesses, but we have One Who has been tempted in every way, just as we are—yet was without sin." (Hebrews 4:15)*

Even in His humanity, Jesus never sinned, never disobeyed the Father, never strayed from God's righteousness and holiness—the only human being to ever be free from sin. Not so the rest of us!

When we compare ourselves to others, who are living clearly wicked, immoral and/or abusive lives, we may think that we look pretty good. After all, we're not robbing, murdering, blaspheming, abusing or living in blatant or obvious wickedness. Compared to Adolf Hitler, or Josef Stalin, or Geoffrey Dahmer, I look pretty decent, don't I? No, I don't, not in the face of God's flawlessness. Compared to the absolute, perfect purity and holiness of God—which is the only true standard by which to judge—we are infinitely far from any reasonable definition of "good."

Preparing to begin a revival meeting in a large city, famed evangelist Billy Sunday wrote a letter to the mayor asking for the names of individuals he knew who had spiritual problems and needed help and prayer. How surprised the evangelist was when he received from the mayor a city phone directory.[82]

We can deny our sin, but that is clearly disingenuous. On some level, I would suggest, we all know the truth. As the apostle said it: *"If we claim to be without sin, we deceive ourselves and the truth is not in us ... If we claim we have not sinned, we make Him out to be a liar and His word has no place in our lives."* (1 John 1:8 and 10)

Some people deny the reality of sin itself—what's wrong for you may not be wrong for me, it's all relative. Others laugh at sin. Flip Wilson made it a punchline by claiming, "The devil made me do it." Still others take pride in their sin. Think Frank Sinatra: "I did it my way!" As one author said it:

> The most dangerous attitude toward sin is to tone down its awfulness. Psychology calls sin maladjustment; biology labels it a disease; ethics suggests that it is a moral lapse; philosophy regards it as a stumbling in the upward progress of the human race.[83]

But perhaps on some level many people, if not most people, realize that they are only fooling themselves.

We constantly read news stories of people who were considered to be outstanding community servants, but who were later discovered to harbor some hidden, heinous sin. There is an old story to the effect that Noel Coward sent identical notes to the twenty most prominent men in London, saying, "All is discovered. Escape while you can." All twenty abruptly left town. They were afraid that their secret sins had been discovered!

I'm not sure if that story is true, but there is no such thing as a "secret sin." God sees and knows it all, and the Holy Spirit of God has come to cut through the fog of our self-justifications, denials and rationalizations and to convict people of their sin, their lack of righteousness and the judgment to come. The wages of sin is death, (Romans 6:23), for *all* of us; that is the judgment that we deservedly face. Unless we acknowledge our sinfulness, we will never truly see our need for a Savior, and we will never trust in Jesus to be our one and only Messiah.

But praise God, the Holy Spirit has also come to convince people that Jesus is the answer to our eternal dilemma.

> *"When He comes, He will convict the world of guilt in regard to sin and righteousness and judgment: in regard to sin, <u>because men do not believe in Me</u> ..." (John 16:8-9, emphasis mine)*

There are many millions who do not believe in Jesus. They think of Him as a wise teacher, a good man, a spiritual guru, a moral example, a prophet, or a faith healer. Others, less charitable, have seen Him as a charlatan, liar, misguided fool, even mad.

But they do not understand who He truly is—the Son of God, second Person of the Divine Trinity, the Savior who died on the cross to pay the penalty for our sins and rose again on the third day. It is the work of the Holy Spirit to convince people of those truths.

In fact, in chapter four we considered the absolute necessity of the regenerating work of the Spirit in all who truly believe. It is only through the Spirit's work of convicting us of our sinfulness and His convincing us of the salvation that comes through faith in Christ that we can believe the Gospel truth. Unless the Spirit of God thus awakens our dead spirits, we are utterly incapable of saving faith. Thanks be to God for His grace!

The Spirit provides this conviction in innumerable ways. He uses our witness and testimony in the hearts of others as we share the Gospel with family, friends, neighbors, classmates and coworkers. He works through the faithful ministry of missionaries and evangelists spreading out across the globe, sometimes in spite of dangers and threats. He uses the Scriptures themselves, as people pick up a Bible, read it and are convinced. He uses Christian radio and television ministries, films, music and books. He even uses dreams. I have read and heard that many in closed, Muslim countries are being converted to Christ when He appears to them in their dreams!

How were you awakened to the things of God? How did the Spirit penetrate your heart and soul, convicting you of your need for a Savior and convincing you that Jesus is the one and only Messiah? Was it a sudden, dramatic conversion experience, or a slow, gradual stirring of your heart? What Scripture passage(s) did He use to arouse your spiritual sensitivity? Who were the people who spoke God into your life and helped you to understand? When did you experience the reality and presence of God, igniting the flame of faith in your heart? Thank God the Spirit for His faithful, patient, regenerating and awakening work in your life!

Perhaps one more point needs to be made about the convicting work of the Holy Spirit. It is not only directed at unbelievers. Believers themselves also and often need the help of the Spirit to recognize their ongoing sins.

King David, a man of faith, a man after God's own heart (1 Samuel 13:14) was deeply convicted of his sins of adultery with Bathsheba and the murder of her husband. Yes, it was the prophet Nathan who boldly confronted David, but it was surely the Spirit of God Who condemned him in his heart, that he cried out:

> *"Have mercy on me, O God,*
> *according to Your unfailing love;*
> *according to Your great compassion*
> *blot out my transgressions.*
> *Wash away all my iniquity*
> *and cleanse me from my sin.*
> *For I know my transgressions,*
> *and my sin is always before me.*
> *Against You, You only, have I sinned*
> *and done what is evil in Your sight,*
> *so that You are proved right when You speak*
> *and justified when You judge." (Psalm 51:1-4)*

It was Daniel, the man of prayer and the prophet of God, used mightily by God in the kingdom of Babylon and among the people of exile, who fell on his knees in prayer:

> *"O Lord, the great and awesome God, who keeps His covenant of love with all who love Him and obey His commands, we have sinned and done wrong. We have been wicked and have rebelled; we have turned away from Your commands and laws. We have not listened to Your servants the prophets, who spoke in Your name to our kings, our princes and our fathers, and to all the people of the land." (Daniel 9:4-6)*

From where did that heart of repentance come in such a godly man if not from the conviction of the Holy Spirit?

This is the work of conviction by the Holy Spirit in the life of a believer. We can merrily go our way in life, oblivious to our disobedience, or at least refusing to admit it to ourselves and to God. But the Holy Spirit will not allow us to do so indefinitely. If we are a believer in Christ, if His Spirit resides within us, sooner or later He will prod our conscience and force us to face the truth.

Our choice then is to repent or to stubbornly continue to deny. But gently, or pointedly, He will continue to urge us to acknowledge the sin and confess it. And when we do so, God is always ready to forgive.

> *"If we confess our sins, He is faithful and just and will forgive us our sins and purify us from all unrighteousness." (1 John 1:9)*

Dr. Karl Menninger, in his book titled *What Ever Became of Sin?* told the story of a sunny day in September, 1972. A stern-faced, plainly dressed man was seen standing still on a street corner in the busy Chicago Loop. As pedestrians hurried by on their way to lunch or business, he would solemnly lift his right arm, point to the person nearest him, and intone loudly a single word: *"GUILTY!"*

Then, without any change of expression, he would resume his stiff stance for a few moments before repeating the gesture. Then, again, the inexorable raising of his arm, the pointing, and the solemn pronouncement of the one word: *"GUILTY!"*

The effect of this strange pantomime on the passing strangers was extraordinary, even eerie. They would stare at him, look away, look at each other, and then hurriedly continue on their way. One man, turning to another, exclaimed: "But how did he know?"[84]

That may be said to have been the beginning of conviction—admitting that there is something to know. And in the case of the Holy Spirit of God, He *always* knows. He convicts sinners of their sinfulness and need for a Savior, and He shows those who already believe the error of their ways. But, thankfully, He does more than simply point and shout out our guilt. He also convinces us of the truth of the Gospel: Jesus died to pay the penalty we deserve and He offers forgiveness and reconciliation with God to all who will believe.

QUESTIONS FOR CONTEMPLATION OR CONVERSATION

1. Have you ever had the thought that it must have been much easier to follow Jesus when He was alive and here on earth? If so, how does it make you feel to hear Him say it would be better for us if He were to leave?

2. Do you think it would be better to have Jesus' personal presence in your life or the indwelling Holy Spirit in your heart? Why?

3. How were you awakened to the things of God? How did the Spirit penetrate your heart and soul, convicting you of your need for a Savior and convincing you that Jesus is the one and only Messiah? Was it a sudden, dramatic conversion experience, or a slow, gradual stirring of your heart?

4. What Scripture passage(s) did He use to arouse your spiritual sensitivity? Who were the people who spoke God into your life and helped you to understand? When did you experience the reality and presence of God, igniting the flame of faith in your heart?

5. When and how has the Holy Spirit confronted you with your sin? How did you respond and what was the result?

6. Is the conviction of the Holy Spirit a positive thing or negative in your mind? Why?

Conclusion

"I have much more to say to you, more than you can now bear. But when He, the Spirit of truth, comes, He will guide you into all truth. He will not speak on His own; He will speak only what He hears, and He will tell you what is yet to come. He will bring glory to Me by taking from what is Mine and making it known to you. All that belongs to the Father is Mine. That is why I said the Spirit will take from what is Mine and make it known to you. In a little while you will see Me no more, and then after a little while you will see Me." (John 16:12-16)

There is, of course, much, much more that could be said about the Holy Spirit of God. We have just scratched the surface in these pages. As I said at the outset, I made no attempt here to write a complete, systematic theology of the Holy Spirit. We simply looked at some of the Bible passages in which God the Father or God the Son spoke directly about God the Holy Spirit.

Hopefully, though, this was enough to pique your curiosity and cause you to pray, meditate and study some more. There are many other Bible passages to which you might turn in an effort to fill in the gaps. (See the appendix.)

The Spirit of God is a priceless gift to us all—convicting us of our sin, convincing us of our need for a Savior, opening our hearts and minds to the things of God, pointing us to Christ as the Messiah we seek and need, and so much more. Thank God for His precious grace to us in Christ and in His Spirit.

As Jesus said to His disciples, we can trust in the Spirit to continually guide us into all that is true and right. When we are open and receptive to

Him, and as we immerse ourselves in God's eternal Word, we will learn and grow in that truth and mature as followers of the Way of Christ. The Holy Spirit has come to aid us in that sanctifying process and to prepare us for an eternity in God's Kingdom.

My prayer for you at this point is that you might humbly submit to the guidance and grace of God the Father, Son and Holy Spirit, and enjoy an ever-expanding relationship with your loving Creator. It all begins when you respond to the wooing and awakening of God's Spirit and believe in Jesus as your personal Savior. There is no other way.

I recently read an old story that told of then 67-year-old Bill O'Brien, who had donated over one hundred pints of blood. He said, "When the final whistle blows and St. Peter asks, 'What did you do?' I'll just say, 'Well, I gave one hundred pints of blood.' That ought to get me in."

Someone wisely commented, "If Mr. O'Brien is counting on giving one hundred pints of blood to get him into heaven, someone ought to tell him he's trusting in the wrong blood." The great old hymn asks, "What can wash away my sin? Nothing but the blood of Jesus."

"In Him we have redemption through His blood, the forgiveness of sins, in accordance with the riches of God's grace." (Ephesians 1:7)

"But now in Christ Jesus you who once were far away have been brought near through the blood of Christ." (Ephesians 2:13)

So if God the Holy Spirit is prompting you, pray to Him today—right now. Confess your sins, admit your need for His mercy and help, accept the forgiveness He offers, and become part of the family of God. The Holy Spirit will take up residence in your heart and bring with Him countless benefits and timeless truth, to help you begin (or, maybe, continue) an exciting journey of faith, from this life to the next. If you need help getting started, maybe a prayer such as this would be a good beginning for you:

Dear Lord Jesus,

I know that I am a sinner and need Your forgiveness. I believe that You died to pay the penalty I owe for my sins. I want to turn from my sins. I now invite You to come into my heart and life. I want to trust You and follow You as Lord and Savior. Lead me in Your ways and make me a faithful follower of God and His Word. Amen.

Endnotes

CHAPTER 1

1. R. Jamieson, A. R. Fausset, and D. Brown, *Commentary Critical and Explanatory on the Whole Bible, Volume 1* (Oak Harbor, WA: Logos Research Systems, Inc., 1997), p. 17.

2. Ibid., p. 17.

3. R. L. Thomas, *New American Standard Hebrew-Aramaic and Greek Dictionaries: Updated Edition* (Anaheim: Foundation Publications, Inc., 1998).

4. A. P. Ross, *Genesis;* in J. F. Walvoord and R. B. Zuck (Editors), *The Bible Knowledge Commentary: An Exposition of the Scriptures, Volume 1* (Wheaton, IL: Victor Books, 1985), p. 15.

5. R. Jamieson, A. R. Fausset, and D. Brown, *Commentary Critical and Explanatory on the Whole Bible, Volume 1* (Oak Harbor, WA: Logos Research Systems, Inc., 1997), p. 17.

6. M. Henry, *Matthew Henry's Commentary on the Whole Bible: Complete and Unabridged in One Volume* (Peabody: Hendrickson, 1994), p. 4.

7. F. Brown, S. R. Driver, and C. A. Briggs, *Enhanced Brown-Driver-Briggs Hebrew and English Lexicon* (Oxford: Clarendon Press, 1977), p. 934.

8. R. Jamieson, A. R. Fausset, and D. Brown, *Commentary Critical and Explanatory on the Whole Bible, Volume 1* (Oak Harbor, WA: Logos Research Systems, Inc., 1997), p. 17.

9. Wayne Grudem, *Systematic Theology: An Introduction to Biblical Doctrine,* (Grand Rapids, MI: Zondervan Publishing House, 1994), p. 241.

10. R. L. Thomas, *New American Standard Hebrew-Aramaic and Greek Dictionaries: Updated Edition* (Anaheim: Foundation Publications, Inc., 1998).

CHAPTER 2

11. R. Jamieson, A. R. Fausset, and D. Brown, *Commentary Critical and Explanatory on the Whole Bible, Volume 1* (Oak Harbor, WA: Logos Research Systems, Inc., 1997), p. 56-57.

12. P. L. Tan, *Encyclopedia of 7700 Illustrations: Signs of the Times* (Garland, TX: Bible Communications, Inc., 1996), p. 272.

13 Y. Choi, *Holy Spirit in the Old Testament.* In J. D. Barry, D. Bomar, D. R. Brown, R. Klippenstein, D. Mangum, C. Sinclair Wolcott, ... W. Widder (Editors), *The Lexham Bible Dictionary* (Bellingham, WA: Lexham Press, 2016).

14 P. L. Tan, *Encyclopedia of 7700 Illustrations: Signs of the Times* (Garland, TX: Bible Communications, Inc., 1996) pp. 521-522.

CHAPTER 3

15 I. Merriam-Webster, *Merriam-Webster's Collegiate Thesaurus* (Springfield, MA, 1996).

16 J. I. Packer, *Concise Theology: A Guide to Historic Christian Beliefs* (Wheaton, IL: Tyndale House, 1993), p. 35.

17 R. Ellsworth, *Opening Up Psalms* (Leominster: Day One Publications, 2006), pp. 125-127.

18 R. Jamieson, A. R. Fausset, and D. Brown, *Commentary Critical and Explanatory on the Whole Bible, Volume 1* (Oak Harbor, WA: Logos Research Systems, Inc., 1997), p. 32.

19 J. I. Packer, *Concise Theology: A Guide to Historic Christian Beliefs* (Wheaton, IL: Tyndale House, 1993), p. 35.

20 M. Henry, *Matthew Henry's Commentary on the Whole Bible: Complete and Unabridged in One Volume* (Peabody: Hendrickson, 1994), p. 942.

21 J. D. G. Dunn, *Spirit, Holy,* in *New Bible Dictionary, 3rd edition* (Leicester, England; Downers Grove, IL: InterVarsity Press, 1996), p. 1128.

CHAPTER 4

22 Warren Wiersbe, *Wiersbe's Expository Outlines on the Old Testament* (Wheaton, IL: Victor Books, 1993), Ezekiel 1-36.

23 M.G. Easton, *Easton's Bible Dictionary* (New York: Harper and Brothers, 1893).

24 George Cavanagh in P. L. Tan, *Encyclopedia of 7700 Illustrations: Signs of the Times* (Garland, TX: Bible Communications, Inc., 1996), p. 1205.

25 D. Martyn Lloyd-Jones, *The Christian Soldier* (Grand Rapids, MI: Baker Books, 1977), p. 34.

26 George Herbert, "The Holdfast," in *English Poems of George Herbert,* ed. Wilcox, p. 499.

27 P. L. Tan, *Encyclopedia of 7700 Illustrations: Signs of the Times* (Garland, TX: Bible Communications, Inc., 1996), p. 571.

28 H. H. Hobbs, *My Favorite Illustrations* (Nashville, TN: Broadman Press, 1990), p. 254.

29 Ibid., p. 255.

30 Scott Christensen, *What About Evil? A Defense of God's Sovereign Glory* (Phillipsburg, NJ, P&R Publishing, 2020), pp. 475-476.

CHAPTER 5

31 John Walton, Victor Matthews and Mark Chavalas, editors, *The IVP Bible Background Commentary, Old Testament* (Downers Grove, IL: InterVarsity Press, 1973), 760.

32 W. W. Wiersbe, *Wiersbe's Expository Outlines on the Old Testament* (Wheaton, IL: Victor Books, 1993), Joel.

33 Ibid.

34 Walter Elwell, editor, *Evangelical Dictionary of Biblical Theology* (Grand Rapids, MI: Baker Books, 1996), p. 420.

35 J. E. Smith, *The Minor Prophets* (Joplin, MO: College Press, 1994), 86-87.

36 R. B. Chisholm, Jr., *Joel*, in J. F. Walvoord and R.B. Zuck (Editors), *The Bible Knowledge Commentary: An Exposition of the Scriptures, Volume 1* (Wheaton, IL: Victor Books, 1985), pp. 1416-1421.

37 R. Jamieson, A. R. Fausset, and D. Brown, *Commentary Critical and Explanatory on the Whole Bible, Volume 1* (Oak Harbor, WA: Logos Research Systems, Inc., 1997), pp. 666-667.

38 H. H. Hobbs, *My Favorite Illustrations* (Nashville, TN: Broadman Press, 1990), pp. 138-139.

39 P. L. Tan, *Encyclopedia of 7700 Illustrations: Signs of the Times* (Garland, TX: Bible Communications, Inc., 1996), pp. 555-556.

CHAPTER 6

40 P. J. Achtemeier, in *Harper's Bible Dictionary*, 1st edition (San Francisco: Harper & Row, 1985), p. 200.

41 W. W. Wiersbe, *Wiersbe's Expository Outlines on the Old Testament* (Wheaton, IL: Victor Books, 1993), Zechariah.

⁴² P. L. Tan, *Encyclopedia of 7700 Illustrations: Signs of the Times* (Garland, TX: Bible Communications, Inc., 1996), p. 507.

⁴³ Ibid., p. 506.

⁴⁴ Ibid., p. 507.

⁴⁵ D. Martyn Lloyd-Jones, *The Christian Soldier* (Grand Rapids, MI: Baker Books, 1977), p. 39.

CHAPTER 7

⁴⁶ M. G. Easton, in *Illustrated Bible Dictionary and Treasury of Biblical History, Biography, Geography, Doctrine, and Literature* (New York: Harper & Brothers, 1893).

⁴⁷ K. Brooks, *Summarized Bible: Complete Summary of the Old Testament* (Bellingham, WA: Logos Bible Software, 2009), p. 212.

⁴⁸ R. Jamieson, A.R. Fausset, and D. Brown, *Commentary Critical and Explanatory on the Whole Bible, Volume 1* (Oak Harbor, WA: Logos Research Systems, Inc., 1997), pp. 732-733.

⁴⁹ Ibid., pp. 666-667.

⁵⁰ *U.S. News and World Report*, April 22, 1996.

⁵¹ P. L. Tan, *Encyclopedia of 7700 Illustrations: Signs of the Times* (Garland, TX: Bible Communications, Inc., 1996), p. 555.

CHAPTER 8

⁵² W. W. Wiersbe, *The Bible Exposition Commentary, Volume 1* (Wheaton, IL: Victor Books, 1996), pp. 36-38.

⁵³ J. P. Louw and E. A. Nida, *Greek-English Lexicon of the New Testament: Based on Semantic Domains, electronic edition of the 2nd edition, Volume 1* (New York: United Bible Societies, 1996), p. 312.

⁵⁴ M. Henry, *Matthew Henry's Commentary on the Whole Bible: Complete and Unabridged in One Volume* (Peabody: Hendrickson, 1994), pp. 1661-1662.

⁵⁵ P. L. Tan, *Encyclopedia of 7700 Illustrations: Signs of the Times* (Garland, TX: Bible Communications, Inc., 1996), p. 522.

⁵⁶ M. Henry, *Matthew Henry's Commentary on the Whole Bible: Complete and Unabridged in One Volume* (Peabody: Hendrickson, 1994), pp. 1661-1662.

⁵⁷ P. L. Tan, *Encyclopedia of 7700 Illustrations: Signs of the Times* (Garland, TX: Bible Communications, Inc., 1996), p. 522.

CHAPTER 9

58 W. W. Wiersbe, *The Bible Exposition Commentary, Volume 1* (Wheaton, IL: Victor Books, 1996), pp. 294-296.

59 M. R. Gordon, *Regeneration*; in D. R. W. Wood, I. H. Marshall, A. R. Millard, J. I. Packer, and D. J. Wiseman (Editors), *New Bible Dictionary, Third Edition* (Downers Grove, IL: InterVarsity Press, 1996), p. 1005.

60 D. Ortlund, *Gentle and Lowly, The Heart of Christ for Sinners and Sufferers* (Wheaton, IL: Crossway, 2020), p. 171.

61 Ibid., p. 61.

62 W. W. Wiersbe, *Wiersbe's Expository Outlines on the Old Testament* (Wheaton, IL: Victor Books, 1993), Ezekiel 37.

63 C. C. Ryrie, *A Survey of Bible Doctrine* (Chicago: Moody Press, 1972).

64 Wayne Grudem, *Systematic Theology, An Introduction to Biblical Doctrine* (Grand Rapids, MI: Zondervan Publishing House, 1994), p. 699.

65 Ibid., p. 701.

66 P. L. Tan, *Encyclopedia of 7700 Illustrations: Signs of the Times* (Garland, TX: Bible Communications, Inc., 1996) p. 571.

67 H. H. Hobbs, *My Favorite Illustrations* (Nashville, TN: Broadman Press, 1990), p. 85.

68 Ibid., p. 85-86

CHAPTER 10

69 W. W. Wiersbe, *The Bible Exposition Commentary, Volume 1* (Wheaton, IL: Victor Books, 1996), pp. 352-353.

70 J. P. Louw and E. A. Nida, *Greek-English Lexicon of the New Testament: Based on Semantic Domains, electronic edition of the 2nd edition, Volume 1* (New York: United Bible Societies, 1996), pp. 141-142.

71 W. W. Wiersbe, *The Bible Exposition Commentary, Volume 1* (Wheaton, IL: Victor Books, 1996), pp. 352-353.

72 P. L. Tan, *Encyclopedia of 7700 Illustrations: Signs of the Times* (Garland, TX: Bible Communications, Inc., 1996), p. 1312.

73 R. Jamieson, A.R. Fausset, and D. Brown, *Commentary Critical and Explanatory on the Whole Bible, Volume 2* (Oak Harbor, WA: Logos Research Systems, Inc., 1997), p. 156.

[74] M. Henry, *Matthew Henry's Commentary on the Whole Bible: Complete and Unabridged in One Volume* (Peabody: Hendrickson, 1994), p. 2014.

[75] W. W. Wiersbe, *The Bible Exposition Commentary, Volume 1* (Wheaton, IL: Victor Books, 1996), pp. 608-609.

CHAPTER 11

[76] M. Henry, *Matthew Henry's Commentary on the Whole Bible: Complete and Unabridged in One Volume* (Peabody: Hendrickson, 1994), p. 2016.

[77] J. Beeke and P. Smalley, *John Bunyan and the Grace of Fearing God* (Phillipsburg, PA: P & R Publishing, 2016), pp. 102-103.

[78] E. Achtemeier, *Creative Preaching* (Nashville: Abingdon Press, 1980).

[79] H. Ross, *The Genesis Question: Scientific Advances and the Accuracy of Genesis* (Colorado Springs, CO: Navpress, 2001), p. 13.

[80] P. L. Tan, *Encyclopedia of 7700 Illustrations: Signs of the Times* (Garland, TX: Bible Communications, Inc., 1996), p. 187.

CHAPTER 12

[81] J. P. Louw and E. A. Nida, *Greek-English Lexicon of the New Testament: Based on Semantic Domains, electronic edition of the 2nd edition, Volume 1* (New York: United Bible Societies, 1996), p. 435.

[82] P. L. Tan, *Encyclopedia of 7700 Illustrations: Signs of the Times* (Garland, TX: Bible Communications, Inc., 1996), p. 1287.

[83] H. H. Hobbs, *Fundamentals of Our Faith* (Nashville: Broadman Press, 1960), p. 64.

[84] K. Menninger, *What Ever Became of Sin?* (Portland: Hawthorn Books, 1973).

Appendix

For further study, see the following Scriptures passages related to the Holy Spirit:

Genesis 1:2; 6:3; and 41:38
Exodus 31:3 and 35:31
Numbers 27:18
Nehemiah 9:20
Job 33:4
Psalms 51:11-12; and 139:7
Isaiah 11:2; 30:1; 42:1; 44:3; 61:1; and 63:10, 11, 14
Ezekiel 36:27
Joel 2:28-29
Micah 3:8
Zechariah 4:1-7; and 12:10
Matthew 1:18; 3:11; 3:16-17; 10:20; 12:31-32; and 28:19
Luke 1:15, 35, 67; 11:13; and 24:49
John 1:32; 3:5, 6, 34; and 6:63
Acts 2:2-4, 33, 38; 4:8; 5:3, 4; 8:15-19; and 10:19, 44-47
Romans 5:3-5; and 8:1-27
1 Corinthians 2:11-14; and 12:3-11
2 Corinthians 1:22
Galatians 4:6; and 5:5-25;
Ephesians 3:5, 16; and 4:3, 4, 30
Philippians 2:1
1 Thessalonians 5:19
Titus 3:5-6;
Hebrews 2:4; and 6:4
1 Peter 1:2; 3:18
2 Peter 1:21
1 John 4:2, 13; and 5:6-8
Revelation 14:13

For more information, see also:

Evangelical Dictionary of Biblical Theology, edited by Walter Elwell (Grand Rapids, MI: Baker Books, 1996), pp. 344-351.

New Nave's Topical Bible, by J. Swanson and O. Nave (Oak Harbor: Logos Research Systems, 1994).

Systematic Theology: An Introduction to Biblical Doctrine, by Wayne Grudem (Grand Rapids, MI: Zondervan Publishing House, 1994), pp. 634-653.

About the Author

As a pastor, Rev. Lenn Zeller served four churches in three states (Ohio, Illinois and Pennsylvania) over a period of thirty-eight years. He also served the wider church on the denominational level in several capacities. Now retired, Rev. Zeller lives in the mountains of Pennsylvania, with his wife and partner of forty-seven years, Janeen, and enjoys a more relaxed lifestyle. That added time has allowed him to write.

This book is the third in a series which looks to God's Word, the Bible, for relevant and reliable information about God Himself. First was *What God Has Said—About God,* then came *What God Has Said—About Jesus,* and now in this volume *What God Has Said—About the Holy Spirit.* In this age of information, with a plethora of sources claiming to know the truth, it is vitally important to verify the information you are receiving as accurate and correct. What better person to turn to than God Himself, in His holy Word? All three books in this series turn to God's eternal revelation for truthful answers about the person and character of God the Father, God the Son, Jesus, and God the Holy Spirit.

ALSO BY LENN ZELLER

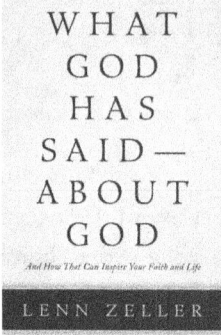

*What God Has Said
—About God*

Available at: Amazon.com, BarnesandNoble.com, Christianbook.com and Westbowpress.com.

*What God Has Said
—About Jesus*

Available at: Masthof.com
and Amazon.com.

www.ingramcontent.com/pod-product-compliance
Lightning Source LLC
Chambersburg PA
CBHW070108080526
44586CB00013B/1225